The Quest for Self-Understanding

UNEASY MANHOOD

UNEASY MANHOOD

The Quest for Self-Understanding

ROBERT HICKS

OLIVER
NELSON

A Division of Thomas Nelson Publishers
Nashville

Published in Nashville, Tennessee, by Oliver-Nelson Books, a division of Thomas Nelson, Inc., Publishers, and distributed in Canada by Lawson Falle, Ltd., Cambridge, Ontario.

Unless otherwise noted, the Bible version used in this publication is THE NEW KING JAMES VERSION. Copyright © 1979, 1980, 1982, Thomas Nelson, Inc., Publishers.

Scripture quotations noted NASB are from the New American Standard Bible, © 1960, 1962, 1963, 1968, 1971, 1972, 1973, 1975, 1977 by The Lockman Foundation. Used by permission.

Printed in the United States of America.

ISBN 0-8407-9125-9

Library of Congress Cataloging-in-Publication Data

Hicks, Robert, 1945–
    Uneasy manhood : the quest for self-understanding / Robert Hicks.
        p.   cm.
    Includes bibliographical references.
    ISBN 0-8407-9125-9 (hardcover)
    1. Men—Psychology.   2. Masculinity (Psychology).   3. Sex role.
    4. Men—Religious life.   I. Title.
    BF692.5.H53   1991
    155.6′32—dc20   91-10557
                                                              CIP

1 2 3 4 5 6 — 96 95 94 93 92 91

To
my father
C. N. Hicks

aviator, corporate manager, skeet shooter,
gun collector, auto mechanic, all-around fixer,
husband, and biggest fan,
known to the world as "Jack"
but to me as
Dad.

Thanks for being my dad
and a man.

"The glory of sons is their father."
A proverb of King Solomon
—Proverbs 17:6 NASB

Contents

——— ■ ———

Foreword

—■—

Like electronic billboards in Times Square, a collage of neon screams out conflicting expectations to men today. Cars, cigarettes, suits, and stereos are all sold as avenues to increased manliness. Manhood is reduced to a rowdy, barroom debate between "tastes great" and "less filling." Male movie heroes face flying bullets with the casual confidence of those who know that the script guarantees in the end the hero will defeat the enemy and get the girl.

On the other side of the street, men's fashion magazines feature models with three-hour hairstyles meticulously primped to look like the men just woke up. "Real" men fill their wardrobes with fine silks, colorful suits, and walls of shoes for every occasion. Mr. Mom has emerged. Sensitivity is the route to a woman's heart. Gender differences are minimized.

Adding to this neon cacophony of media expectations and role models, wives may have another list: knight in shining armor, servant, counselor, personal Rambo, baby-sitter, teddy bear, chef, and automatic money machine.

In the midst of confusion, most men have retreated. Defeated by trying to follow models of male competence that exist only in Hollywood, alone without close male friends, and woefully inadequate in relationships with females, modern men hear a great deal of criticism but little constructive help. It is from this gaping canyon that *Uneasy Manhood* is written.

Yet *Uneasy Manhood* is not a male version of the popular psychological books that exist in dump truck loads on issues such as women's assertiveness, overcoming codependency, motherhood in the 1990s, and the working mother. This is a man's book written with the illustrations and concrete, hard-hitting realities that a man needs. It is not a book about five easy steps or three secret gimmicks. It raises direct issues. It doesn't provide simple solutions because most of us know that none exist. It does, however, provide some sensible steps for a man to begin to take charge of these issues in his own life and lay the groundwork for a healthy understanding of maleness in the lives of his sons.

Bob is a close friend and wholly, eminently qualified to write this book. As an Air Force Reserve officer, he's seen that countries, wives, and children need protectors. As a husband of Cinny, he knows that maleness is best seen in the context of femaleness. As a father of three teenage children, he knows that raising children in today's world is not a task for cowards. As a professor in higher education he knows all the theories, but as a counselor he knows which ones don't work. As a biblically-centered theologian, he draws upon the wisdom of God and provides answers that pierce beyond the physical and emotional to the depth of the problem in the spiritual realm.

It is probably in this last category where this book is most profoundly unique. True healing begins at the root of male spirituality, and Bob is a trustworthy guide. You are invited to join him in what may be a tough but rewarding journey.

—Howard G. Hendricks
Chairman, Center for Christian Leadership
Distinguished Professor
Dallas Theological Seminary

Acknowledgments

———— ■ ————

Having dedicated this work to my father, I must also recognize many others who had a significant part in the writing process. I thank my mother for being so understanding in the raising of her son. You, Mom, were always there, putting up with me and supporting all the "male things" that young boys and adolescents get into. Thanks for all the meals, clean clothes, and irrational commitment you demonstrated through my trek toward manhood.

I also appreciate my second family for giving up their husband and father for days at a time in order to produce this volume. They are truly my inspiration. Without their understanding I would not have been able to write about such personal issues at all. Charis, Ashley, and Graham, my treasures from the Lord, you are outstanding, each of you, in your own way in spite of the father you were given. Thanks for being the great kids that you are. Cinny, you are the fairest of all. From day one of our married life, you believed I could write. Thank you for your self-sacrificing support of me and your support through the crazy process of writing a book that never seemed to get finished. Even though I know you don't believe it, I am not worthy of you. I have truly found a good thing!

ACKNOWLEDGMENTS

Most of this book was written at the Jersey shore, overlooking the rough Atlantic in the winter and the beautiful Stone Harbor park in the summer. Without Bob and Debbie Blum's place at the shore, I am convinced this book would not exist. Thanks, Bob and Debbie, for providing an easy place to write about an uneasy subject.

I would also like to thank my publisher for believing in the project. Thanks go to Vic Oliver for his timely suggestions and commitment.

Introduction

———— ■ ————

I know men. For the past forty-five years I've been one! During the last twenty-some years, I've worked with them in the military, the banking business, the ministry, and higher education. I've talked with them all over the world. I've listened to them on fishing boats in Fiji, on sheep-shearing stations in the outback of Australia, over brown bags in employee lunchrooms, and in prestigious lunch clubs in Honolulu, Dallas, and Philadelphia. I've listened to their concerns, fears, and frustrations. I've sat with them through the deaths of loved ones, through the complexities of bankruptcies, court-martials, marital affairs, and loss of jobs. I've prayed with them, laughed with them, wept with them, and shared innumerable breakfasts and lunches with them. This book is one extended conversation, a conversation that makes one statement: manhood doesn't come easily . . . if it ever comes at all!

When I first thought of writing a book on this subject, I casually mentioned it to my secretary. Being quite single, she announced, "I hope you call it *Men Should Come with Instructions*." Her comment was pregnant with insight. The masculine side of life is often misunderstood or not given the opportunity to be understood by the other gender. Women, it seems, have the advantage of mutual self-talk, the kind of talk that reveals the inner self and instantly puts women on the same wavelength.

> *Men do not begin to deal with issues of manhood until they encounter certain vocational, marital, or parental problems.*

Men can be the beneficiaries of this feminine self-talk if they listen. On the other hand, men do not talk as openly about their issues as women do. The result: manhood takes on a greater mystique than the other sex ever dreamed. Today, almost any university of significant size offers courses, if not a whole department, in women's studies. Subjects on men's issues are rare. Most colleges do not list one course on anything to do exclusively with men. Yet, most men I know do not feel slighted by this omission. They carry on, wanting neither to engage nor to enrage the feminists while at the same time not realizing there are many attitudes, misconceptions, biases, and myths concerning manhood about which they have never had one serious conversation. In my experience, men do not begin to deal with issues of manhood until they encounter certain vocational, marital, or parental problems. Then their unique male approaches or difficulties in relationships bring them face-to-face with their uneasy manhood.

The subject matter of these chapters is not the result of a large-scale research project. In fact, the original outline came to me while listening to a boring sermon one Sunday morning. (See chapter 8, "Uneasy Sundays.") At least Sunday morning sermons give men a lot of think time they otherwise would not have! However, the chapters reflect the issues men have told me they most struggle with. To confirm my assessment of men's issues, I have taken a survey of various men's groups and through a bimonthly men's letter I write. These responses have been very helpful in determining whether I was on target and the degree to which some issues might be problematic.

I have tried to write as a fellow traveler on this journey toward manhood. I have tried to express what so many have felt they could not express to wives, employers, pastors, and friends. In this regard I write as their advocate . . . an advocate for their feelings and perspectives. I do not desire to kindle the flames of antifeminism or to set the sexes against each other. My deepest desire is to bring the sexes together through understanding and reconciliation. As a marriage counselor, I have felt for years that men need to better understand women and women need to better understand men. That's the only way marriages can become stronger. But the advantage has gone to the women because they talk more. Therefore, more is known about women's inner life and feelings than about men's.

I hope this book will fill a gap in helping women better understand men and men better understand themselves. The goal is to provide some of the instructions my secretary so desired about men. Whatever benefits men may appear to have in our culture, I contend the road to manhood is not an easy one.

Men today are angry about their limited options concerning their roles compared to those of women. *Time* magazine devoted its fall 1990 special edition to women's issues. The edition was entitled "Women: The Road Ahead." The last article in the magazine—"What Do Men Really Want?"—was an addendum. In this tacked-on essay Sam Allis notes,

But in the wake of the feminist movement, some men are beginning to pipe up. . . . They are airing their frustrations with the limited roles they face today, compared with the multiple options that women seem to have won. Above all, they are groping to redefine themselves on their own terms instead of on the performance standards set by their wives or bosses or family ghosts. . . . In many quarters there is anger. The American man wants his manhood back.[1]

This book attempts to bring some of these frustrations to the surface so that they are on a conscious level for both men and women. Through the process, I have not tried to "fix" anything. As an advocate for men's feelings and frustrations, I do not believe that is my task. Also, I am skeptical of any book that claims to "fix" the massive social complexity of men's roles and issues. Other books can offer their five-step solutions to men's problems, but that has not been my goal. My purpose is to illumine, examine, and ask for understanding of this thing called manhood . . . a manhood that is not easy.

gle with manhood. I love my son, but I hate the category marked behavior on his report cards. Graham's social ability has never measured up to a teacher's expectations. During one parent-teacher conference when it was suggested we send our son to a special resource room for individualized instruction, I asked, "I'm curious. How many girls are sent to this room?" The teacher quickly responded, "Very few." "Hmm," I said, "there must be some behavioral or intellectual difference between boys and girls!" I'm not sure the teacher appreciated my "rationalization." Was I excusing my son's behavior? Of course not. He does get into trouble. But did my statement about male differences have any validity? Maybe our problems with manhood today begin with childhood and the way our society, even the church, approaches the education and nurture of boys.

Feminization of Nurturing Institutions

I suggest that there has been an increasingly large-scale feminization of the major nurturing institutions since World War II. The amount of time boys spend with women as compared to the amount of time boys spend with men through the first twelve years of life is severely disproportionate. I am not trying to make these issues of right or wrong; I am merely observing the reality of the situation. Because men go off to work for the most significant hours of the day, and they rarely pursue careers in early or elementary education, male-to-male contact has been minimized. Add to this trend the divorce rate and the current divorce laws that favor giving custody to the mother, and boys have very little contact with grown men. Now that mothers are entering the workplace in growing numbers, the nurturing functions are left to child-care facilities or home-care arrangements headed and staffed predominantly by women. Women have always cared for boys in the early years, but men were also there in the home. For much of early history, only men were teachers. Now, both situations are different. Men are not at home, and they are not involved in the early years of education.

The church is not immune to this trend. I have known churches that would never let a woman teach men (grown ones), but throughout their children's department in Sunday school, they have nothing but women teachers. (It is usually easier to recruit the women than the men, to the men's neglect!) From a child development perspective, a child is much more influenced by this instruction than an adult. Yet, the concern for church leaders is more with women's teaching adult men than with the overall impact of women's teaching on boys. Hence, even at church, boys are taught, disciplined, and administered largely by the opposite gender.

A "Few Good Men"

When I was a pastor in Hawaii, my little congregation was near Kaneohe Marine Corps Air Station. I always had a large supply of muscular recruits. The young, mostly single marines had great hearts but not much tact. When out of uniform and away from their sergeant, they just stood around waiting for someone to tell them what to do next. At one of our Sunday school complaint sessions, several women teachers described their discipline problems with the young boys. They couldn't control them for the hour-long Bible lesson. They had tried everything and were ready to quit. I had a flash of insight. I grabbed a couple of marines and told them to go into those rooms the next Sunday, pile a couple of boys under each arm, "rough them up, and sit on them." To the women, that strategy bordered on child abuse, but the boys viewed it as affection! Our discipline problems were solved by placing one marine per room with the order to pile his lap full of boys and then hold them while the teacher taught the lesson. In one Sunday I came to realize every pastor needs a "few good men"!

I work with a psychologist who used to be an employee of the

Philadelphia public school system. Over lunch one day I asked him, "What percentage of problem kids you saw were boys?" He laughed and revealed what was common knowledge among educational psychologists. "About 80 percent," he replied. I have asked schoolteachers the same question: "Who are your most problematic kids . . . boys or girls?" The response, usually accompanied by laughter, is the same: "Boys, of course!"

In one study of child gender disorders ("Gender Identity Disorders and the Family," Dr. George Rekers), the researcher concludes that "the literature deals almost exclusively with the cases of deficit masculine development." Look at early reading problems, dyslexia, or behavior control. Again, boys have most of the stats. John Guidubaldi, professor of early childhood education and director of a study, noted,

> Far more detrimental effects of divorce are on boys than on girls. . . . Boys are much more affected by their parents' divorce because children fare better with single parents of the same sex, and 90 percent of all custody rights go to mothers. Out of 341 children from divorced families in the study, fathers had custody in only 24 cases.[1]

One might conclude from the data that being a boy growing up in today's culture places one at great risk, especially in school. Stanford researcher Diane McGinnis observed, "There seems to be a conspiracy among mothers, teachers and physicians to keep normal, testosterone-loaded, active males medicated at school in order to keep them quiet."[2]

Teachers, Grades, and Brains

Why do boys do so poorly or at least less well than girls? I contend that there are three reasons: teachers, grades, and brains. First, who are the first teachers in the child's experience? Women! What kind of students do they like best? Girls!

Yes, girls, who stay clean, sit where they are supposed to, color within the lines, love homework, especially math, and hate pushing and shoving. Elementary schools were made for little girls. Consequently, they generally do better than boys, who are more into playground, spit wads, frogs, and a model of a "Top Gun" F-14 than their map of the United States. Boys don't quite fit the system; therefore, they get into much more trouble.

> One might conclude from the data that being a boy growing up in today's culture places one at great risk, especially in school.

A second reason is grades. Boys are also at a great disadvantage compared to girls when grading comes around. In the early elementary school years, girls' cognitive reasoning ability develops faster than that of boys. Girls have a slight to great edge in the abstract thinking areas, which include subjects like language facility and math. The problem is that during this time, boys excel in areas involving physical coordination, and most school systems give letter grades to the abstract thinking areas and only satisfactory or unsatisfactory ratings to physical activities. It doesn't take long for a boy to see that an unfair game is being played, one that makes it difficult for him to win or just be acceptable to school systems or educators.

A certain irony surrounds this problem. In regard to grading, evaluating boys with boys and girls with girls would be more fair. And if we extend the logic further, having separate classes for girls and for boys would be indicated. Here lies the irony. The Catholic parochial and private prep schools had the right idea all along, but they had little research to support their approaches.

With the advent of the civil rights movement and women's rights, the veil separating the boys' schools from the girls' schools was rent down the middle. Now Bryn Mawr has men, and Swarthmore has women. The changes that came were argued not on the basis of research or learning theories but on the basis of pure civil rights. Now the research is available to suggest . . . guess what? Men learn differently from women, and boys especially learn differently from girls. The reason: their brains process information in different ways. Dr. Peter Blitchington, a professor of psychology, has noted,

> Surprisingly, the few studies that have been conducted on the question have shown that children in sexually segregated classrooms, i.e., those who are taught in a classroom with a teacher of the same sex and class members of the same sex— boys with boys and girls with girls, do better academically and show more satisfaction with the school system than children who are taught in coeducational classrooms.[3]

Thus, the third reason boys are at a disadvantage in elementary school is that their brains and girls' brains process information differently. With the split brain experiments in the late seventies, a new field of study was opened. The first studies revealed how one side of the brain communicates data to the other side and integrates the information into a complex to be understood by the person. These studies have taught researchers about many of the differences between how men and women, boys and girls, learn. Even in the womb, the male brain begins to develop differences (from week sixteen to week twenty-six).

During this time, the brain responds to the XY chromosome, and a certain washing of the left hemisphere leaves the male brain unfinished. The connective tissue that unites the two sides of the brain, called the corpus callosum, in males has fewer nerve endings, which makes for less effective lateral transmission between the halves. As a result, males have a certain deficiency early on in language ability, abstract thinking, linear functions, and math facility—basically, what elementary schools major in and what girls love.

Dr. Richard Restak, in his best-selling book *The Brain*, writes,

On the basis of the information already available, it seems unrealistic to deny any longer the existence of male and female brain differences. . . . Over 95% of hyperactives are males. The male brain learns by manipulating its environment, yet the typical student is forced to sit still for long hours in classrooms. The male brain is primarily visual, while classroom instruction demands attentive listening. Boys are clumsy in fine hand co-ordination, yet are forced at an early age to express themselves in writing. Finally, there is little opportunity in most schools, other than during recess periods, for gross motor movements or rapid muscular responses. In essence, the classrooms in most of our nation's primary grades are geared to skills that come naturally to girls but develop very slowly in boys. The results shouldn't be surprising: a "learning disabled" child who is also frequently "hyperactive." . . . We now have the opportunity, based on emerging evidence of sex differences in brain functioning, to restructure the elementary grades so that boys find their initial contacts less stressful.[4]

If the school system isn't going to give boys a break and make their trek toward manhood a little kinder, where can they get the understanding they need? One would think the answer would be the institution of the home. But it can also be harmful to boys and make their manhood uneasy.

Inaccessible Fathers

Harvard family researcher Armand Nicholi has said, "Human families constitute the vital cells of the body we call society. . . . The strength of the families determines the health of the nation. The disruption of the families not only imposes a vast economic burden on the state but inflicts on individuals more sorrow and suffering than war, poverty and inflation combined."[5] This being the case, who is affected the most when families break up . . . boys or girls? Again, the literature suggests boys, especially when dad has been lost as a significant player in the boy's life. The increasing number of inaccessible fathers in our culture may be one of the most harmful causes of the improper development of boys. In the Rekers study, the boys who were classified as the most profoundly disturbed shared father absence. Nicholi notes that father absence for long periods contributes to low motivation for achievement, inability to defer immediate gratification, low self-esteem, and susceptibility to group influence.[6]

> **The increasing number of inaccessible fathers in our culture may be one of the most harmful causes of the improper development of boys.**

Following a Harvard study of men with MBA's who had spent ten years in the business world, a researcher wrote, "The interviews I have had with men in the thirties and forties convince me that the psychological or physical absence of fathers from their families is one of the great underestimated tragedies of our times."[7]

With father absence compounding almost daily, the male child is left with his mother or mother substitutes most of the time. Because many of them are single mothers who carry the financial burden of the family, they frankly have little time to be understanding of male development. Like their feminine teacher counterparts, they merely want "peace and quiet" so they can get through the day. As one teacher expressed to me, "All education is reduced down to getting through the next hour and trying to keep the kids under control."

Without an educational system that understands boys, a church that allows for them, a father who affirms them, or a mother who sees beyond their dirty clothes and acting out behavior, boyhood is very uneasy. An uneasy boyhood makes for an uneasy manhood. It is no wonder that men are not doing well in our society. Herb Goldberg states, "By every critical statistic, in the area of longevity, disease, suicide, crime, accidents, childhood emotional disorders, alcoholism, and drug addiction, men show a disproportionately higher rate [than that of women]."[8]

The problem with manhood is boyhood. But men do grow up, at least physically. They leave home, graduate from college, and get jobs; most eventually "settle down." However, when they marry, their manhood makes for an uneasy union, and every man sooner or later must face the reality that his wife will never be totally pleased with him.

CHAPTER 2

Uneasy Union

Or Why Wives Are Never Satisfied with Their Husbands

———■———

I'm your classic baby boomer. Born in 1945, I'm sure I was a not-so-subtle celebration of World War II's wind down. My era was populated with heroes who were larger than life— Generals Eisenhower, Patton, and MacArthur, and the highly decorated soldier Audie Murphy. My generation was the first in history to be nurtured on technicolor images. If World War II heroes were larger than life, television and movie images became colossal figures around which many of our expectations for manhood were built. For boys and girls, John Wayne, the Lone Ranger, Hopalong Cassidy, Randolph Scott, and Sergeant Preston of the Yukon became what true masculinity should look like. I remember reenacting many of the movie plots I had seen; I was, of course, the good guy rescuing, protecting, and fighting. I dressed like my heroes, talked like them, and had the same kind of gun they carried. My backyard became the frontier, a snowdrift was my fort, and the neighborhood girls were the innocent victims to be rescued.

Then someone threw me a curveball. The fifties and sixties took my heroes away. The softer Cary Grant and Rock Hudson changed the image a little, and then with the publication and proclamation of *The Feminine Mystique,* women began to say they wanted more sensitive males. It was a period of clashing images for the male species. Men continued to marry, but divorce rates doubled during the same period. The uneasy issues of manhood resulted in many uneasy unions between husbands and wives. Current divorce rates reveal just how uneasy they were and continue to be.

Clash of Images

The clash of images profoundly affected the expectations of both husbands and wives. Differing expectations based on these conflicting images created many problems for both men and women throughout the seventies and eighties. It is now time to address what has caused such a large-scale disillusionment with marriage and at the same time such an increasing marriage and divorce rate. Ours is simultaneously the most marrying and the most divorcing culture in the world. What are some things that have made marriage for men an uneasy union?

First, we must face the reality that the old images of manhood were myths. Who were those men we watched on TV and at the movies? They were nothing but celluloid! One writer comments, "To model oneself after another man is in itself problematic. But to model oneself after an image of a man, repackaged for the camera, is dangerous. In comparing themselves to the dashing figure riding off into the setting sun or racing across the goal line, ordinary men in everyday life cannot help to feel overshadowed."[1] Even real-life heroes such as Eisenhower and Patton we now know as men who were not necessarily larger than life; they were leaders who made mistakes and were far from perfect.

But the myths of manhood die hard. I am the product of two myths. One myth is that true manhood is evidenced by being the lord of the castle and the provider for the household. The other is that a woman now wants a sensitive, vulnerable husband. (Yes, I believe this is a myth as well.) On the one side, men in our culture are no longer the undisputed lords, breadwinners, and heroes. The Victorian image of lord protector and provider is today a joke except among a few tradition-oriented Christians who try to find that model in the Scriptures. Yet, it is an image I was raised with, identified with, and saw modeled by my father and in the culture at large.

Different Culture

> *Our culture has largely rejected the image of manhood that we cut our teeth on, and the one that on an intellectual level we may admit is Victorian or bigoted.*

Many of us are now caught in a developmental bind. Our culture has largely rejected the image of manhood that we cut our teeth on, and the one that on an intellectual level we may admit is Victorian or bigoted. But at the same time, the new image of the caring, sensitive, Alan Alda-type male feels very uncomfortable for us. Consequently, when we enter marriage, most men experience manhood somewhere between John Wayne and the Alda types. What's worse, our wives want both but rarely admit it! That's why they will never be satisfied with us, and we will never be able to totally please them. John Wayne is dead, Alan Alda is either too threatening or too unbelievable.

One reason for this bind is that our culture is radically different from that of our forefathers. Mark Gerzon observes,

> My father was a biochemist, not a woodsman. Men were commuters, not cowboys. I carried a tennis racket, not a rifle, and wore Arrow shirts, not buckskin. The only Mustangs and Colts I rode were made in Detroit. The only Indians I knew played baseball. Instead of wilderness, there were shopping malls. Dodge City was a cut rate car lot.[2]

Different Expectations

With the change in the culture, our expectations about the institution of marriage also changed. In the past, marriage was one of several institutions where meaning was found and intimacy needs were met. In today's world, marriage has become autonomous. It has turned in on itself. Marriage is the only place left where most people can look for intimacy and companionship. As a society of nomads ever chasing our careers, we have sealed ourselves off from our extended families. Most of our friendships are job related rather than neighborhood related, and the average couple are left to fend for themselves in this modern jungle.

The result is a horrendous expectation to have all one's needs met by one's spouse. A woman looks to her husband to be both lord protector and provider while she also desires and expects him to be a sensitive man, able to read her mind. In addition to these marital expectations are the currently popular expectations for the man to be more involved in the parenting process.

The man must be successful in his work and in his marriage and ever available for duties around the house. If he is not, he can expect to hear various accusations: he is not really committed enough to his work and family, he needs to become a better manager of his time, and/or his priorities are all wrong. Some people love to add another condemning comment: if he can't handle all these things at once, he might not be "walking with God."

One man told me, "Between my boss, my wife, and my kids, at least one of them is mad at me every day for not being at something." A psychiatrist confessed that a man will not begin to change until he comes to grips with the "endless, impossible binds under which [he lives], the rigid definitions of his role, the endless pressure to be all things to all persons, and the guilt-oriented, self-denying way he has traditionally related to women, to his feelings and to his needs."[3]

In counseling, I sometimes use a technique to highlight this masculine dilemma. I say to the woman, "Now let me see if I am hearing you right. [Women love that statement because I am being the caring, sensitive man they want their husbands to be.] You want your husband to be more on your wavelength, to anticipate your feelings, to engage in more girl-type talk, to love shopping and so forth?" She usually responds by saying, "Yes, that's right. That would be wonderful." I reply, "Well, you should have married a woman!" The point is usually clear.

Sensitivity or Strength

Many women want men to be more feminine, but if they will admit it, they still want men to be strong in accordance with the older image. That's quite a bind for men! Women want men to be strong when they need strength, but they also want sensitive, caring males when they need those qualities. And of course, men have to guess which women want or need at any given moment. The ladies can't have it both ways.

A good friend of mine related a conversation with his wife that illustrates the point. The couple had been in marriage counseling, and the counselor had focused on the husband's inability to communicate feelings. Making some of the first attempts to share his feelings with his wife, he took the plunge over dinner one night. In answer to his wife's question, "Something's wrong; what happened at work today?" he opened up instead of saying "nothing" in his typical male fashion.

He responded, "Our company is facing a hostile takeover that may phase out fifty people in my department, one of which may be me. I went to lunch today with some of the people in my office to talk about it, and all the time during lunch this young secretary kept rubbing my leg with her thigh. By the time lunch was over, my mind was racing about how good she would be in bed and how wonderful it would be to run away with her. I also received a phone call from Johnny's principal about his grades, and I fear he may have gotten in with some kids doing drugs. By the way, I lost half our investments on the stock market today."

He said his wife looked at him and stated evenly, "Are you kidding?" He stood his ground: "It's all true." She then went stark raving mad!

Men who have tried to become the more sensitive male have often found that either this isn't what women want or they don't like the implications. In the *Time* article quoted earlier, a Yale psychiatrist presented these insights:

> Men aren't any happier in the '90s than they were in the '50s. . . . Unfortunately, the men who attempt to explore those riches of inner lives often discover that their efforts are not entirely welcome. The same women who complain about male reticence can grow uncomfortable when male secrets and insecurities spill out. . . . I think a lot of women who want a husband to be a typical hardworking bread-winner are scared when he talks about being a sensitive father.[4]

In the past, men kept a lot of what was going on in their personal lives deep inside or confided only in a few other men. Women had their sewing circles and over-the-fence neighbors. Life tended to be separated by men's business and women's talk. But no more. Now the husband is expected to relate to his wife on the intimate feeling level.

Here's the rub. If men are now expected to do this because they love their wives and want to promote the psychological health of the marriage, women must be able to handle the things men share. If a man's fears make his wife more fearful than the situation deserves, he probably won't continue to share his fears.

A primary male feeling is anger, and men have had to learn to control their anger to be socially acceptable. But when the hidden rage of men is expressed to women, it is usually condemned.

Women can't have it both ways. If they want feelings, they are going to get male feelings, given and articulated in distinctively male ways. Women must learn to accept male feelings for what they are, no more and no less. Men have had to learn to accept female feelings for what they are. A woman's rejection of a man's feelings is just as counterproductive as a man's rejection of a woman's feelings. Feelings are not necessarily moral issues that need to be judged; they need to be listened to, understood, and considered significant.

> *Feelings are not necessarily moral issues that need to be judged; they need to be listened to, understood, and considered significant.*

We men also have unrealistic expectations about marriage. We are often angered for having the expectation of lord protector and provider placed on us. At times we get tired of the responsibilities associated with these images, especially when we think our wives may not be leveling with us. They say they want sensitivity, but do they secretly want us to be ambitious and successful at work?

Do women really want a more sensitive male instead of the workaholic, successful-at-work-and-unavailable-at-home male of the past? Again, the *Time* article reveals an intriguing issue:

—— 33 ——

What's going on here? Are we looking at a backlash against the pounding men have taken? To some degree, yes. But it's more complicated than that. The sensitive man was overplayed, explained Seattle based lecturer Michael Meade, "There is no one quality intriguing enough to make a person interesting for a long time," more important, argues Warren Farrell, author of the 1986 best seller *Why Men Are the Way They Are*, women liked Alan Alda not because he epitomized the sensitive man but because he was a multimillionaire superstar success who also happened to be sensitive. In short, he met all their performance needs before sensitivity ever entered the picture. We have never worshipped the soft man, says Farrell. If Mel Gibson were a nursery school teacher, women wouldn't want him. Can you imagine a cover of TIME featuring a sensitive musician who drives a cab on the side?[5]

We men may be accepting an unrealistic and impossible role for ourselves by thinking our wives want what they really don't want. They really want us to be rich and famous. Isn't that the program they either watch or want to watch? Who reads *People?* But can all men be successful at work? Add to that the increasing pressure to be successful in our relationships at home, and it is more than many men can handle.

We men have unrealistic expectations for our wives. There are times we wish our wives would be more responsible for their own lives, make financial contributions to the family, and be the mother at home for both our kids and us. That's an equally unfair and unrealistic bind for them. They cannot be Helen Gurley Brown, Cheryl Tiegs, and Mother Teresa all wrapped up in one energetic package. These are phantom images that do not exist.

Most of us, both male and female, are mediocre marriage partners, trying to do the best we can with the resources we have available. Mediocrity has never sold well in our culture, however. We all want the perfect marriage and the perfect kids, or at least we want to have a growing marriage, which means that it's getting better every year. But how close to reality is this image? I suggest we have far too many expectations for marriage, expectations that continue to destroy often normal, mediocre marriages that would do fine if the spouses didn't know marriages somewhere were doing "better."

A businessman humorously told me, "I hate to see my wife reading another book on marriage because all it does is heighten her expectations for what our marriage ought to be . . . and I'm the guy who always has to pay the price." Despite his humor, he raises a serious issue. Have all these books, tapes, seminars, sex therapies, and marriage enrichment weekends produced any more successful marriages than the generation before us? I am not qualified to evaluate it, but I certainly believe someone needs to question whether even the best of helps has only created more impossible expectations and demands. Is this only a new myth of marriage that doesn't exist anywhere—and one that may only heighten the woman's dissatisfaction with her present experience of intimacy while placing an unreasonable load of guilt on the man so that he feels he will never please his wife?

Men Are Men and Women Are Women

Another issue we as men must face is that men are men and women are women. We must give up the myth that there are no differences. There exist critical differences that cannot be ignored or explained away. When God made Man, male and female, He meant business. The creation order established that maleness is not femaleness and femaleness is not maleness. This distinction seems so basic, but every time I speak on the subject and make this statement, someone (usually a woman) gets upset over it. Ever since the publication of *The Feminine Mystique* in 1963, our culture has sort of pretended there are no more differences between the sexes. Men should do dishes, change diapers, and become housekeepers, while women should learn to change the oil, plan a hostile takeover, and fly jet airplanes.

When the civil rights movement began, women's rights followed in the political wake and successfully argued the case for equal rights. I believe this movement brought about some very necessary corrections. However, politics does not change physiology, neurology, and biochemistry. The equal rights movement was based on civil rights legislation, not on human development research. Changing laws is not the same as changing human nature.

Since the civil rights movement, researchers have rolled up their sleeves and studied such things as male-female differences. One Harvard researcher, Carol Gilligan, has noted that "women bring to life a different point of view and order in human experience."[6] Her illuminating study pointed to essential differences between men and women in their view of relationships, their perception of reality, their basic self-concepts, and their outlook on moral dilemmas. As a part of her study, men and women viewed pictures of men and women in social situations. She writes, "As people are brought closer together in the pictures, the images of violence in the men's stories increase, while as people are set further apart, the violence in the women's stories increases."[7] Her conclusion: women view closeness in positive ways; men view it as violence. On the other hand, women view social distance as abandonment, but men view it as safety.

Brain research explains many of these differences. Dr. Restak observes,

Recent psychobiological research indicates that many of the differences in brain function between the sexes are innate, biologically determined and relatively resistant to change through the influences of culture. . . . Girls differ in their approach to gaining knowledge about the world. They tend to favor a "communicative mode" asking others, taking advantage of other people's experiences, sparing themselves the need to personally encounter all the objects in their environment. For this reason, girls tend to conform by relying more on social cues. Since they are also better equipped in the auditory mode, they can pick up significant information from tones of voice and intensity of expression. Thus, interpersonal skills appear at an earlier age and form the basis for the "communicative mode" most women maintain throughout their lifetime. . . . When it comes to psychological measurements of brain functioning between the sexes, clear, unmistakable differences emerge. In eleven subtests of the WAIS, only two subtests reveal similar mean scores for males and females. When it comes to personality characteristics, males and females tend to show some surprising differences. In four studies on curiosity, three found males to be more curious, one found no differences. In tests of field dependence, girls were found more field dependent than boys in a total of eight cultures. Girls are less likely to take risks, more likely to do well in school and do better under stress.[8]

These differences in brain functioning are simply the male and female hormones doing what they do best. The sex hormones, determined at conception by the chromosomes, program the brain to organize itself along either male or female patterns. What poets and novelists have known for centuries is now confirmed by much scientific research. What God revealed in the first chapter of the Bible is experienced every day between a man and a woman in marriage. The diversity was created for the purpose of bringing about a certain unity in the context of differences.

However, another myth has been perpetuated in both the Western culture and the Christian church: that the statement "they shall become one flesh" (Gen. 2:24) should be understood to mean that individual personalities and differences are somewhat lost when entering this union. Therefore, one personality must be lost in the other's. In past history, usually the wife's personality got lost in her husband's vocational world, but perhaps now the husband's personality often gets lost in the emotional life of his wife. The goal is for neither to lose the self in the other but to be what they are . . . masculinity and femininity living together in unity.

We men view the world differently, and we should not apologize for it. We are what we are . . . men. In response to the feminist agenda, perhaps we have gone too far and capitulated our manhood. One writer suggests that in the sixties, "This country's testosterone got poured out the window, and men have lost their boldness."[9]

> We have to ask ourselves, "Is this new liberated male in reality only a feminized male, who in showing greater openness of feelings has become more like a woman?"

We have to ask ourselves, "Is this new liberated male in reality only a feminized male, who in showing greater openness of feelings has become more like a woman? I do not hear the counterbalancing voices saying to women, "Become more like men. Be responsible. Make something out of your lives. Move on." Many women I know who have tried it don't like it and desire now to go back to the womb of their husband-supported home. Sam Allis remarks,

> As always, men are defined by their performance in the work-place. If women don't like their jobs, they can, at least in theory, maintain legitimacy by going home and raising children. Men have no such alternative. . . . The message is that if a man takes paternity leave, he's a very strange person who is not committed to the corporation. . . . You're still either a master of the universe or a wimp.[10]

James Dittes writes, "Women are not the enemy, nor the present problem, neither are they the solution. . . . However, giving in to the pressure of the new man and living up to the new specifications is at least as deadly as living up to the [older] traditional specifications."[11] I agree.

Our differences do not mean that we men cannot be good marriage partners, desire intimacy with our wives, or be more involved in the parenting process. They do mean that when we devote ourselves to these areas, we will approach them distinctively as men. Women must learn to value and appreciate our approaches, just as we have had to learn to accept and value their distinctive contributions in the work force. As an air force reserve officer, I have learned to value and rely upon the distinctive insight from female officers. Their addition to the officer corps has strengthened the air force. At the same time, when I cook a meal, drive to a new destination, or go shopping, I will never quite do it the same way a woman would. As the movie *Three Men and a Baby* illustrates, a man will not even change a diaper or dry the baby off the same way a woman would.[12]

Therefore, a wife must learn to be pleased with her husband's efforts. My wife has had to accept the fact that I will never park the car where she would have!

Our differences make for uneasy unions, but they are not insurmountable. Women will never quite be pleased with men because they really want a womanlike man. When they find one, they turn around and call him a wimp because he won't stand up to them. We live somewhere today between the John Wayne and Alan Alda images. We know both are unrealistic. We have had to sadly part company with our heroes.

It's quite a bind being male and married. Your wife might still want some combination of Hopalong and Rock Hudson, but both are dead. Most men will never be like either one. Most of us will never be Rambos or Schwarzeneggers. From their bodies to their billfolds, we are not them.

But what do men want from the women in our lives? Sam Allis concludes his article, by saying

What do men really want? To define themselves on their own terms, just as women began to do a couple of decades ago. "Would a women's group ask men if it was OK to feel a

CHAPTER 3

Uneasy Buddies

Or Why the Beer Commercials Make Some Men Feel So Good

——■——

Wally and I were buddies. He was the quarterback; I was the fullback. He played forward; I was the point guard. He played left field; I was the catcher. We were the only three-sport lettermen in our graduating high-school class. We had gone through junior and senior high together, double-dated, worked out together, played pool together, and worked on cars together. Then he went to the University of Kansas and I to Kansas State. Apart from two or three college breaks, I never saw Wally again. In high school, we appeared inseparable. Since high school, we have been separated for good. Were we friends? Of course we were friends! We were the kind of friends men have: friends of convenience, location, and common achievement, friends one can walk away from and never see again.

Need for Friends

For men, even our friendships do not come easy. They are complicated, rarely evaluated, and never talked about. In the final analysis, once we marry and have kids, if they don't happen with the people we work with, they probably will never happen at all. But our need for friends or our need to romanticize about friends is our common yearning. That's why most men see themselves in the beer commercials, and that's why the commercials make men feel so good. Some men may toast glasses of Chablis with their dates, but they may drink beer with their buddies. Men dream of having friends like the ones on the beer ads. There we are drinking together after the rugged soccer or softball game, reliving the game and enjoying one another's company.

But are the TV portrayals of men watering at their favorite pub true portraits of reality? Probably not. But if they are fantasies, why do they sell so well? A New York psychiatrist suggests, "You've seen those beer commercials. . . . That's not the way men are together or ever were, but it's the way they think they were and that's all that matters. Two men may be sitting at a bar and saying one word every ten minutes, but in their minds they're in one of those beer commercials."[1]

The fantasy is deeply rooted in the American collective conscience. In one study of American literature, the researcher asserts,

The romanticized image of friendship between males has been a central image in American literature. . . . The reoccurring themes include male friends, often of different races, moving away from women, the family and the community into the wilderness whether that be the forest, the ocean, outer space, or the inner city. The resourcefulness of the men and their loyalty or love for each other is tested and deepened by a series of challenges, often culminating in an act of violence. This fantasy of male brothers finding fulfillment outside relationship with women and the family pervades American culture.[2]

So the fantasy feeds the manhood issues for men. On the one side, they have deep-seated needs for friends, but on the flip side, there are many binds for men in both initiating and cultivating deep relationships. Many are left looking for the friend they can never have, or the friend they thought they once had, while they face a host of factors making friendship uneasy.

Away from the Responsibilities of Home

My wife values friendships with other women. Several times in our twenty-some years of marriage I have had to watch from the sidelines the mutual intimacy she has enjoyed with good friends. I have often wondered if that is possible for me or if it is just something women enjoy when they "click" with one another. I feel the uneasy bind. Somehow women do not have to give up family, husbands, or work to be close with other women. But for men, our history of friendship takes us away from the responsibilities of home, family, and marriage. In fact, it takes us away from responsibility, period! Our friends are Vietnam vets, work buddies, and golf partners, but the turf where we play is always a safe distance from the home. This absence creates an automatic tension along with the charge from the wife that we are "acting irresponsibly" by spending so much time with our friends.

> For men, our history of friendship takes us away from the responsibilities of home, family, and marriage. In fact, it takes us away from responsibility, period!

One Dallas wife was suspicious of her husband's time with

a friend. Gradually, the evenings spent with his friend were more frequent and lasted later. She wondered what was really going on. Her husband's explanation was that they were having severe problems at the office and they needed the time together to work things out. She wondered, *Which is it, another woman or is he gay?* When she finally pressed him about how long it would take to work out the problems, he confessed, "Ed and I go out not to solve anything but to drink and forget about the problems!"[3] They were building a friendship around avoiding, not sharing. And that is the male's way. To his wife, he was being irresponsible—and in a certain way he was—but it was his way of coping with something he couldn't deal with, and he had a buddy who understood it and was a part of it.

Taken to the extreme, this man will probably either keep using alcohol as an escape mechanism with destructive results or give up his friend and start acting responsibly again by going home. Yet, the story illustrates the nature of male relationships. They take place not as shared articulated values but almost purely by accident. After studying male friendships among veterans, Margaret Mead wrote,

> The closeness of men under fire was not based on mutual interests, or shared emotions, but on solidarity in the face of danger. It was arbitrary, undiscriminating closeness. Inevitably, they were bunkmates, tank mates, or foxhole mates. These special relationships were accidents of association not based on special personality characteristics and therefore were not capable of ripening into real friendship.[4]

Men have a better understanding of what we like in a woman than we do in a man. Most men do not notice when another man walks into a room or a restaurant, but we are very aware (whether we show it or not) of every woman who enters. We rarely talk about the traits in men we admire or the qualities we would like in a friend. I cannot remember ever having those questions asked of me by another man, even while talking about the subject of friendship. For men, friend-ships happen, or they don't. When they don't, we pay a high price.

High Cost of Male Friendship

The reality is that men today feel more comfortable with women than with other men.

Recent studies suggest the male's friendlessness exacts a high cost in both physical and psychologi-cal health, especially in old age. Some research-ers are currently calling men's difficulties with friendship a major social problem in our culture.[5] The reality is that men today feel more comfortable with women than with other men. This probably is explained by the fact that when we were boys, our early care givers and teachers were all women; add to that the large-scale father and strong male absence and it is no wonder men feel more "at home" with women. Dr. Joseph Pleck notes, "The modern male prefers the company of women because they are primary validators of masculinity."[6] A Washington, D.C., psychiatrist said, "Women who think that men's friendships with other men are somehow better than their relationships with women simply don't know enough about friendships between men."[7]

Why Friendships Are Difficult

Why are friendships so difficult, and why do they make our manhood so uneasy? David Smith in his excellent book *The Friendless American Male*[8] suggests several reasons. First on his list is our aversion to showing emotion. I love the scene in the movie *Brian's Song* where Gale Sayers stands up before a group of people and tells the world that he loves his dying friend and fellow teammate Brian Piccolo. Out of our male homophobic fears, we have lost appropriate ways of expressing our love, appreciation, and emotion for other men. I stand in awe of other cultures where men can embrace, kiss, and express emotion apart from any homosexual suspicion. To make manhood less difficult, a man needs to take the risk of trying to tell a friend how much he loves him or how deeply hurt he was by something said.

A second barrier is a man's inability to value friendship apart from any utilitarian purpose. Women call my wife and ask her to go to lunch. She says, "Great," and that's that. They do lunch. But men must invent reasons to go to lunch. If there is not a reason, the man who is being asked is a little suspicious. We have to say, "There's something I want to talk to you about, or I want to run a business deal by you, or let's play golf on Thursday." But never, absolutely never, would a man say, "I so appreciate you and like being with you. Let's go to lunch."

As a pastor, I have found that working around this barrier is difficult. I've gotten together with men just to get to know them better, but after two meetings, they say to me, "What is it you want? Does the church need some money or do you want me to teach Sunday school or what?" I usually respond, "I just want to see how you are doing." Some look puzzled. One looked me straight in the eye and said, "I don't have time for this!" At least he was honest and knew where he was in his life. A couple years later his company was on the verge of bankruptcy, and he then appreciated a pastor who desired to know how things were going with him.

Smith's third barrier to male friendship is inadequate or nonexisting role models. Men are torn between two extremes. On one extreme are the many mythologies of friendship as seen in the tight bonds of Huck Finn and Tom Sawyer, Tonto and the Lone Ranger, Butch Cassidy and the Sundance Kid, or the Dukes of Hazzard. On the other extreme are the distant, cordial but cold relationships so common between men. How many of us have actually seen close male-to-male friendships? Our fathers were not known for them, and what about our grandfathers? At the same time I must ask myself, What am I modeling to my son? Does he see me as a friend to any other man? I hope he has and will continue to do so, but I fear I send him confusing messages. My son has asked me on several occasions in the past few years, "Dad, who is your best friend?" Why do I feel I am lying when I mention a name? I somehow know the connection he is making in his unsophisticated brain, "If he is Dad's best friend, why does Dad never spend any time with him?" Ouch! It's hard to value another man in this culture for no other reason than that you enjoy being with him. The list of men I really feel comfortable around and enjoy being with is very short.

The fourth thing that makes friendships difficult, even with men I might enjoy getting to know, is the inordinate competition between us. Somehow beyond puberty, men are constantly evaluating themselves by how well they appear to be doing in the eyes of the other men. I suggest that men have a basic winner-loser philosophy of life. The philosophy runs this way. There are losers in life, and there are winners in life. If you want to be a winner, you have to look like a winner—whether you are or not. Being perceived as a loser is the worst possible situation for a man. Therefore, in all his relationships, a man must be on his guard to always appear a winner. If he shares too many weaknesses during a certain period of time, another man will begin to consider him a loser and separate from him because he doesn't want to appear to be a friend of a loser.

I've seen this happen many times. A man loses his job and has to cut back on eating out, loses the club membership, and can't take the annual skiing trip with the wife. Finally after being out of work for a year, he has lost all his friends. At some point, the "friends" began to see him as a loser and separated from him.

It happens on the way up as well. Several men I know attended the same college, went into business at the same time, and belonged to the same church. Their wives were all close.

Some have done well in business, but others have struggled and never "quite made it." The ones who have not made it feel less masculine, less like men, than those who have made it.

Do friends intentionally want their lower-status friend to feel like a failure? I don't believe so, but he often feels that way because of the others' success. In a performance-driven society, even our friends are formed around socioeconomic status.

Therapists have observed this dynamic:

> When men seek therapy, a number of gender issues often may affect the therapeutic process. Asking for help in our culture often leads men to feel inadequate. Not only is it unacceptable to have problems, but it is also "unmanly" to seek help from anyone, and especially from other men.[9]

> *In a performance-driven society, even our friends are formed around socioeconomic status.*

Viewing other men as threats in light of one's own weakness breeds a very uneasy manhood!

My wife and I conduct marriage retreats. One of our most well-received illustrations is our conflict over driving. She always wants to ask directions; I never do. The illustration always brings responsive laughter that reveals the inner conviction and universal guilt. What is it about men that we refuse to ask for help until it's too late? I'm furious if I have to stop and ask a convenience store clerk for directions! (They never know how to get there anyway.) For my wife, it's second, if not first, nature. The best argument I've heard for women's spiritual leadership is the humorous commentary on the biblical experience of Moses in the wilderness. The line goes: Who else but a man would have wandered around in a circle for forty years without asking for directions?

Mask of Normalcy

Whether it's a problem with marriage, the kids, or our own health, we hide our incompetency and out-of-controlness behind a mask of normalcy. This is the fifth reason why friendships are difficult. This tendency has a detrimental effect on male friendships. Two men will play a game about who they are and how well they are doing when in reality they are dying.

I remember being with a group of men who had just been through a devastating work experience together. A psychologist was helping them "process" the experience. He threw out the first question: "What is your reaction to what happened?" There was silence for what seemed like a long time, then one man spoke. He simply and shortly said, "It wasn't all that bad." I knew from individual counseling and conversations that some men in the group were really hurting. But the first man had spoken for the group. Since he was well-esteemed by the group, everyone followed suit. It was as if the rest of the men concluded that by revealing a weakness in front of this man, the others would view them as less masculine, less competent, even less spiritual, and not quite up to par. Finally, though, one man said, "I'm not doing real well. In fact, this experience just about destroyed my family." His opening of the inner door gave the other men permission to open theirs, which they did.

Men have problems asking for help, and they must be given permission to do so. But it takes some men who will not view the request as calling into question their manhood or competency or state of the soul.

The Friendship Magic

Like the man I mentioned who didn't have time to develop friendships, many men place no priority on forming male-to-male relationships. There is no way I can convince these men that friendship is important. I cannot make men feel what they do not feel or what they do not want to feel. But I do know that I have tasted a small sample of what the friendship magic is all about. It's the three-hour lunch where the waitress finally hands you the dinner menu. It's your friend stepping into your office at 2:00 P.M. and saying, "Let's get out of here and take in a movie." It's laughing at a funny magazine at 11:00 P.M. until you think your sides will split. It's having to tell your best friend that his wife has cancer because she doesn't have the courage to tell him. It's listening to a brother who confesses he just doesn't know how to make his wife happy. It's hearing the heartrending confession of your friend's affair when you love both him and his wife. It's being there when a man's daughter dies or when he goes to court or when he goes home to his Maker.

> **We can hide in the closets of competition, use the walls of women to protect us, or flee from the reality of our deepest fears, but when we do, we flee from our own manhood.**

We can hide in the closets of competition, use the walls of women to protect us, or flee from the reality of our deepest fears, but when we do, we flee from our own manhood. The close, non-sexual presence of other men will affirm our manhood more than anything else. Through these encounters, we validate our experiences as men, lose our deep-seated dependency on women, and find the same-gender counterpart we need who truly understands what it is like to be a man. Dr. Ken Druck notes, "Having established ourselves as a man among men, we build confidence and free ourselves to trust others in close relationships." He also points out,

> Studies have shown that men with at least one close friend in whom they could confide about themselves and their

problems had, in effect, a buffer against such crises as the loss of a wife or job, a chronic illness, and the psychological stresses of aging. In terms of their morale and health, these men have a significant edge over men who lack a close confidant.[10]

The tragedy is that so few men have experienced the friendship of other men. In Daniel Levinson's classic study of men, he concludes that men in their early and middle adulthood need to work on certain components of life structure. If their developmental work is to be successful throughout life, an important task during this time is forming mutual friendships. He says,

> In our interviews, friendship was largely noticeable by its absence. As a tentative generalization we would say that close friendship with a man or woman is rarely experienced by American men. . . . In general, however, most men do not have an intimate male friend of the kind that they recall fondly from boyhood or youth. . . . We need to understand why friendship is so rare and what consequences this deprivation has for adult life.[11]

I don't miss some of the jobs I left but I do miss the friends. Barry, I miss you. You taught me that it's OK to be crazy. I learned to laugh "in the Spirit" with you. I enjoyed your going to sleep during afternoon movies, your heart for people, and your inquiring mind that always refreshed me. Thanks for your Jewishness and the love for your people that you gave me. I miss you. Fitu, Jan, and Morris, I can't believe I left you guys for career reasons. In some ways, you made Hawaii the best years of my life. We went through much together. You learned the Scriptures from me, and I learned about politics, fishing, and Hawaiian life from you. No, I learned about *life* from you. Those were good years, and I miss the Ohana spirit I shared with you. Thanks for letting a Houle into your life. To Rick, Tom, and Jon, I'm glad I still have you to dump on.

Rick, your creative musical talent makes me stand in awe, but I most value your friendship; Tom, thanks for being there through a lot of pain, not as shrink but as friend; Jon, I value your honest daring to cut through so much of the institutional and personal foolishness that surrounded a period in our lives.

As I read the above list, I notice most of the names have fallen around my vocation. We men usually develop our friends where we work. Having a friend makes my manhood easier, especially when it comes to this thing called work. However, the work itself does not make my manhood any easier. The paycheck never comes easy.

CHAPTER 4

Uneasy Paycheck

Or Why Men Work the Way They Do

———■———

I can't remember too many discussions with my father about the subject of work. He was like most men of his era. He went to work in the morning and came home at night, some days earlier and some later. The only times I remember his being at home during the day were when he was sick, and those times were rare. I do, however, remember the one thing he said to me about the subject of work. I don't remember the context or whether I asked for it, but his matter-of-fact statement is still with me after all these years. He said, "Son, I don't care what you do. Just don't work for a corporation!" Dad did. He worked for the same company for forty years. From four decades of labor, my father had developed a view of work wrapped in the simple package of "don't." Well, I haven't worked in the corporate world yet, but I have worked for several organizations that approximate the same experience.

Somehow, almost all work today has become corporatelike. Even the ministry is similar to the corporate jungle. The church has its unique brand of well-intentioned dragons who go after people's jugulars in ways that would make corporate executives shudder.

Traditionally, work has been the turf of men, but now that the arena has yielded to the other sex, men have had to rethink the meaning of work and begin to think through a host of new work-related issues. Since work occupies one-half of a man's waking hours, this area of life is critically important. For an activity claiming so much of our time, we ought to reflect more on its nature, essence, and meaning.

In this sense, work is like the air we breathe; we are not really aware of it until we are out of it. Most men don't think about the nature of work until they lose their jobs. Work for us (and for women now, also) has taken on paramount social significance. Some would say it is the sum total of social and personal significance for men.

Social etiquette used to dictate that one say, "How do you do?" Today, "How do you do?" has been replaced by "What do you do?" The question gets at the bottom line for most men. Their identity is closely tied to their work. When work is going well, they do fine. Let the job go poorly, and many fall apart or suffer in many other ways. In our culture, being unemployed means being perceived incompetent.[1] Other men are becoming increasingly dissatisfied with their work, even when they have it and are good at it. A current bestseller states,

> **Social etiquette used to dictate that one say, "How do you do?" Today, "How do you do?" has been replaced by "What do you do?"**

For one thing, many workers in the modern marketplace feel increasingly bored with their jobs and with life. This is the subtext of all the glitzy beer, hamburger, and travel commercials that show hardworking laborers building America and solving its problems. They portray the workplace not as it is but as we wish it could be—an engrossing, challenging, even uplifting human drama in which each of us performs our strategic role and fulfills a personal mission. Instead, for many work is "just a job." Its value begins and ends with a paycheck.[2]

For most of the men I've known, including myself, work does not come easy. Whether the take-home is large or small, the paycheck is not an easy one.

Why We Work the Way We Do

Getting men to evaluate why they work the way they do is next to impossible. They just work, do what is expected of them, whether they like it or not, find some outside enjoyable pursuits, and hope to put in enough years to get their pension and a gold watch. But to a new emerging group, often called yuppies or older baby boomers, the reasons for working are not the same. They differ radically from those of my father's time. Understanding how this historical shift has come about may be helpful.

Historical Overview of Work: Economic Reason

For most of the world's history, work has been an economic necessity. In rural, agricultural societies there were no other options. If one did not work, he literally did not eat. Work was a survival issue. If the crops failed, one borrowed from a neighbor, moved to where there was food, or starved. Many in our world today live at this lowest level. They work to live. By comparison, people in the Western world do not work to have food, even though the numbers of homeless and starving increase daily. Most of us reading this book do not work to have food. Our government still provides food stamps to those who may really need it. Let's face it. We work for other reasons.

Economic Security

I'm only one generation away from the economic reason for working. My parents saw their parents suffer much during the Great Depression. Dad dropped out of school in the eighth grade to help support the family and himself in the way he desired. But as the world wars came to an end, the economic necessity reason gave birth to another philosophy of work centered on economic security. For a generation raised with the insecurities of the Great Depression, it seems the whole next generation focused on giving families the things denied them.

This postdepression and post-World War II era generated the unbelievable American dreams of home ownership, money in the bank, and a car in every garage. Suburbia was alive and well due to the hard-working industrial-managerial corporate complex that supplied the worker "security" in exchange for his faithfulness to the company and his hard work. Survival motives were traded for security issues. Men worked for the secure world that had been denied them.

At this point, I must insert a tribute to my own mother and father. I stand in amazement at what my parents did. My father, a junior-high dropout, self-educated himself, went back to night school, and became the first accountant for a major aircraft corporation. He educated three kids through college and graduate school. And he always, always, had at least one hundred-dollar bill in his billfold (always frustrating his son, who just needed a dollar!). He invested money wisely and worked to retirement with many comforts. During the same time, my mother was at home raising me and my two sisters, packing our lunches in the morning, picking us up after school, and being supportive and caring through all my teenage years. I have been the unconscious beneficiary of my parents' security. As a result, I think I am a reasonably secure person within myself. For this, I owe my parents and their philosophy of work an everlasting thank-you.

Personal Significance

Working for security died, at least temporarily. The generation that had everything began working for other reasons. The baby boomers and yuppies wanted more out of life than a gold watch and a reliable washing machine. They worked for personal significance. The movement from an industrial society to a technological society created the drive for finding more meaning in work than work could ever provide. *Achievement, recognition, status, style,* and *affluence* became the "hype" words of the seventies and eighties. A bumper sticker on a Dallas Mercedes sums it up: "He who has the most toys at the end of the game, wins." (Notice the masculine pronoun!) Today's generation works for its toys, Rolexes, BMW's, trips, and a cabin at the lake.

> *"He who has the most toys at the end of the game, wins." (Notice the masculine pronoun!)*

The women in this generation, if not working for these things themselves, at least expect their husbands to provide them as tokens of their love. Often, the church has placed an uncritical blessing on this relationship. The man's role is to be the primary provider, and the woman is to be the faithful helpmate and worker at home. The result is that she finds her significance in her husband's significance. It's quite a bind for a man having his own significance come from his work and also his wife's significance riding on his. This is often more than some men can bear. In fact, the longer men are unemployed, there are usually two identity crises created by the unemployment—his and hers. She finds much of her identity in his career and success. The burden of finding significance through work makes a man's manhood uneasy.

Theological Reasons

Whether we realize it or not, the church has mothered many of the positions or views concerning the subject of work. Men work the way they do because they think it is the way God or the church wants them to work. In this regard, men have gone from seeing very little divine value in their work to expecting their work to be a unique calling from God.

According to the first view, man's work is second-class labor. This view has historical roots in the Bible. From the creation of the nation of Israel as God's people (Ex. 19—20), God divided the people into priests and laity. The priests got to serve God, while the rest got to serve Moses! Not really, all were to serve God, but the worshipers had to approach God through the sacrificial system administered by priests. The ones who really did God's work were the priests; for the rest, work was not divine work.

This view was sustained until the time of Christ. Jesus came and broke down the division between the sacred workers and the people (Matt. 27:51; 1 Peter 2:5). However, traditions are hard to break, and by the fourth century A.D., the division between the sacred work of the priests and the secular work of the rest of the people was resurrected. It stood until the time of Luther and the Reformers in the sixteenth century, when they tried to give the ministry back to the layman. Though they were successful in giving the priesthood back to all believers, they perhaps gave the people a view of work that in the long term became just as problematic.

In reaction to the medieval position that considered priests the only ones called to the work of God, Luther regarded all work as a calling from God: "In making shoes, the cobbler serves God, obeys his calling from God, quite as much as the preacher of the Word. God himself will milk the cows through him whose vocation it is."[3]

That position was certainly an improvement over the medieval one that granted no divine dignity to common or lay work. However, some have argued that introducing the concept of calling to all work has produced an overvaluation of work that borders on glorification, if not deification. The Protestant work ethic of serving God ultimately became the Puritan work ethic of working hard. With time, the ethic of working hard created a glorification of work in God's name. One writer labels this perspective a vice:

> Work becomes a vice. It is pure and simple an escape mechanism from the anxieties of life. Work can be an escape from family tensions. It can be a device to overcome inferiority complexes. It can, in its final stage, become an escape from oneself and even from God. When it does, let's call it what it is—a sin! The reason why workaholism is a more difficult sin to deal with than alcoholism is that society reinforces it rather than condemns it. The Protestant ethic makes the hard worker the paradigm of virtue and even comes up with biblical and theological justification for it. Work is so respectable that some will have a very difficult time in accepting the thesis of this essay, namely that it can become a vice.[4]

The overvaluation of work, Harvey Cox believes, began in the church. He writes,

> The modern religious sanctification of work began in the medieval monasteries. Unlike Oriental monastic orders, the Benedictines prescribed work as a spiritual discipline. Their cloister bells sounded not just to call the brothers to pray together but also to summon them to common work. The Reformers closed the monasteries, but they did not throttle the monastic spirit. They merely loosed it into the whole society. With Luther, as Max Weber once wrote, the whole world became a monastery and every man a monk. The bells moved from the monastery to the tower of City Hall. The chimes now called not cloistered monks but worldly monks to the disciplined toil which became first the Puritan and later the secular substitute for religious devotion. Even today some people refer to the trade manual of

their professions as its "bible" and speak of working at a job religiously.[5]

Consequently, many men in our culture believe it is their Christian duty to work hard and thereby fulfill their vocational calling at the deepest spiritual level. But in so doing, their Christian life often falls under the dominion of work. I know many Christian men who think their Christian duty is complete if they don't cheat on their taxes, don't swear at work, or don't act on the feelings they have toward the secretary. In return, they can throw all their effort into work and be as successful as anyone else. They can work as many hours as they or the company desires and be viewed as real paradigms of Christian and vocational virtue. In reality, they have made work their god and removed themselves from the scrutiny of the lordship of Christ.

Everything about our work must be placed under the dominion of Jesus. All must be constantly evaluated: the nature of the work itself, the use of the profits by the company, the ethics as they relate to product information, truthfulness in sales presentations, financial accounting practices, and responsibility to stockholders. All these fall under the lordship of Christ for the Christian. Tom Sine speaks about this noncritical view of vocation for the Christian:

One aspect of this attitude toward Christian vocation is a remarkably noncritical view of secular employment. Any job is viewed as being as good as any other job for Christians, as long as they work hard, are honest, and say a little word for Jesus when the opportunity arises. How did we get into such a fix? Where did we get such a naive view of work as it relates to Christian vocation? This attitude stems from the sixteenth-century reformers, who taught that all jobs should be done to the glory of God. And unquestionably this is true; all human activity should be done to the glory of God. But the problem with this doctrine of Christian calling is that not all human activity is synonymous with the biblical concept of vocation, nor does it promote God's agenda. There are life decisions, jobs, and personal goals that are at best irrelevant and at worst diametrically opposed to God's intentions in history.[6]

In reality, comparing the nature of work in Luther's world with our marketplace today is like comparing a home-grown potato with a microchip computer. There is no comparison! Work today cannot be compared with work in any rural or agriculture-based society. Jacques Ellul remarked,

> It is possible to make a meaningful comparison between the fifteen-hour workday of a miner in 1830 and the seven-hour workday of 1950. But there is no common denominator between the seven-hour day of 1950 and the fifteen-hour day of the medieval artisan. We know that the peasant interrupts his workday with innumerable pauses. He chooses his own tempo and rhythm. He converses and cracks jokes with every passer-by. Exactly the same holds true for the qualitative nature of life. . . . We cannot say with assurance there has been progress from 1250 to 1950. In so doing, we would be comparing things which are not comparable.[7]

What Is Work Anyway?

When I graduated from seminary in Dallas, Texas, I went from a running-through-airports pace of life to a slower-paced Polynesian culture of Hawaii. In the early years of that ministry, I was often frustrated because the Island didn't move at the pace I wanted. A Samoan brother and I often had lunch, usually a three-hour one! His counsel was always the same: "You Houles [Caucasians] come over here and do the Houle Hustle. You need to lie down under papaya tree and watch the airplanes fly over. Don't you know God put fish in the sea and papaya in the tree? He takes care of you." I never had an answer for Fitu. His view of work was radically different from mine. But which was better? Which was more Christian? It depends on the kind of life you want and how you apply certain biblical passages. Let's face it. In the Western world, work has taken on some problematic and differing meanings.

As I was writing this chapter, I took a lunch break and went to my favorite deli for a pastrami sandwich. While doing some light reading over lunch, I became aware of the conversation next to me. One man was telling his friend he was not going back to work that afternoon. He said his son had a game at 4:30, and he had done enough work for the day. I quickly realized his view of work was radically different from mine. He was obviously a tradesman (I could notice by his clothes and the truck he drove), and to him, work was something he did. To me, work is a place where I put in time. I could tell a friend, "I'm not going back to work" (which would probably get me in trouble) because work to so many of us has become confined to a place, whether we are working or not! Firemen are at work, even though they may be playing cards. A tradesman is working if he is performing his skill, no matter where he may be. Many men are still at work when they are at home because work occupies their minds.

The definition of *work* is up for grabs today. *Webster's* lists fifteen different meanings. Words like *work, profession, occupation, employment, vocation, career, job,* and *trade* are all used somewhat interchangeably as if they mean the same thing.

One author defines *work* as "Job, occupation, career, trade, profession or whatever is simply a part of work to be negotiated with an employer or one's customers or clients, to provide a useful function in society and an income on which to live."[8]

A simpler statement might be that work is whatever we do to sustain ourselves in the world. From this definition, it should be clear that work involves far more than a mere job or occupation. It involves our goals, our time, our motives, and ultimately our view of life and ourselves. We can blame scientific management theory for departmentalizing the concept of work and making it so organized, rationalized, quantified, and measurable. For the assembly line workers and the men cloistered in little boxes called offices, the dignity of the worker and the nature of work itself have changed, and not necessarily for the better.[9] Consequently, many today seek a job that will not only provide a living but also bring a greater sense of human dignity and enjoyment. Is this so wrong?

Work as Enjoyment

I know a former Seattle architect who loved to vacation in Hawaii. He and his wife planned to retire there. After one splendid visit to the Islands, on the plane ride back they worked out a ten-year plan to transfer their work to Hawaii. By the time the plane landed in Seattle, their ten-year plan had become a one-year plan. As it turned out, they moved six months later. My friend said, "I finally realized I could draft a blueprint anywhere in the world. I didn't have to do it in a high-rise office." He wanted a life with more enjoyment. It was still work but work of a different sort. Was that wrong?

The Holy Scriptures suggest that enjoyment as a motive is not altogether selfish. Solomon observes that in light of the brevity of life, enjoyment of one's labor is not only a good portion for one's life but also to have it is to have one of God's precious gifts (Eccles. 5:18–19). Passages like that reveal it is not wrong to enjoy work or to seek enjoyment in one's work. Enjoying what we spend so much time doing every day is truly a gift from God. That may be why the direct sales industry is one of the fastest growing phenomena in America. Many men are getting tired of working for others with so little enjoyment or profit.[10]

But to place a benediction on enjoyment is not to say that God has placed His favor only on pleasurable labor. He has also placed His favor on the poor and the ones who struggle and face severe trials in their work. If you find pleasurable work, enjoy it as a gift from God. If you don't, you still have the responsibility of supporting yourself and your family. This, too, is pleasing to God.

Work as Productivity

Many men take the highway of productivity. One boss told his employees, "Either produce or reduce." The ones who got reduced were the nonproducers. The ones who produce the most in sales, profits, or best quarterly reports are the ones considered hardworking and most valuable to the company. This pragmatic view of work sees success in measurable, obtainable, and quantifiable terms. This view of productive work feeds our identity and self-image. We are good workers if our work produces something tangible and observable. Performance ultimately determines our decisions, structures, and goals.

Persons perceived as less-productive workers, such as artists, support personnel, and dreamers and thinkers, must constantly face identity crises and the criticism of not amounting to anything. Work as performance creates an approach to work whereby performance dictates who is successful and who isn't. It becomes the god of our vocational value system. Bill Hendricks and Doug Sherman comment,

> A man might be a virtual alcoholic, his second or third wife may have just walked out on him, his kids might be on drugs, and his subordinates might hate his guts—yet if he is successful in his business, we still regard him as a successful person. In fact, he likely thinks of himself that way. And why not? People still crave his endorsement, his money, his name, or his participation.[11]

Unfortunately, the church often follows suit. Look at the leaders in almost any white, upper-middle-class suburban church. Guess who gets to become the leaders? Look at our most trusted Christian organizations. Glance at the letterheads that often list their board members or boards of reference. I am still waiting for an organization to have enough courage to print on the letterhead, next to the businessmen, professionals, and pro football coaches, a plumber or a union boss. Let's face our failure here. We haven't seriously looked at or applied what James has to say about favoritism (James 2:2–4).

I once asked a businessman why we didn't have any blue-collar people on our church board. Without blinking, he said, "They're not leaders." Considering all the white-collar crime and the lack of ethics of many leaders of our business community, I wonder how much serious thought he has given his statement. I don't think that the gift of leadership is confined to persons wearing a certain color collar. I've observed many blue-collar tradesmen supervise workers with such care and skill that certainly they have more qualifications for leadership than many white-collar professionals I've seen. The only reason we prefer the white-collar types is that we in the church view them as successful by the same criteria that the world judges them.

What has driven this uncritical view of success? There could be many reasons, but for some men, their performance is driven by something very subtle.

Work as Something to Prove

Mark Twain said that a boy at age twelve starts imitating a man and goes on doing it for the rest of his life! Twain's quip is psychologically insightful. For years I have listened to men, counseled them, and tried to help them through various developmental crises. And one thing has surfaced many times. There is a lot of unfinished business with these men's fathers and early mentors.

Whatever the views of manhood in our brains, the images have been determined by our fathers and early mentors. They are the ones we looked to early in our experience to define for us what this thing called maleness or manliness is all about. It now frightens me to think that I have a son looking to me to define it for him!

But the point here is that many men use work to prove something to themselves, their fathers, or early mentors about their own manhood. Work becomes a proving ground to long-deserted mentors and fathers.

> **Many men use work to prove something to themselves, their fathers, or early mentors about their own manhood.**

They try to prove to their early mentors that they can make it even when those mentors thought they were losers. A variation on this theme is trying to be as good or great as some mentors who believed in them.

In a Harvard Business School study, grads twenty years out in the field were interviewed. The study concluded that most of the successful top executives still had unfinished business with their fathers. Driving their ambition and goals was work as something to prove. Samuel Osherson points out,

> There are numerous circumstances in adult life that leave us feeling childlike—needy, helpless, powerless to change things. In growing up men have great difficulty coming to terms with dependency and vulnerability, often because our fathers showed us that such feelings were unacceptable, that to be successful men, to win our fathers' approval, achievement was what counted. Our vulnerability and dependency became papered over by an instrumental, competent pose as adults or by focusing on what we do well: our ability to achieve in the work world.[12]

Osherson describes one successful man's view of work as it related to his father:

> Becoming a man felt like accepting an odious burden of endless work and mindlessness. How I would have liked to

talk to my father about that fate, but couldn't or wouldn't!
He was so busy, so tired, so depressed, taking care of us all,
bearing up so well in the arduous male world, for which my
high school was merely the training ground. . . . The biggest
lesson I learned from my father was that, day after day, he
endured. You took what life gave you and you gritted it out.
You were able to get the job done, and he was doing all that
for us, and that is my obligation to him, to take all the [gar-
bage] that life can hand out.[13]

I have been amazed by the numbers of men working hard in
an unconscious attempt to please their dead or distant fathers.
To them, work has become the proving ground of their manhood. One man told me the first time his father called him a
man was when he returned from Vietnam and his father saw
him in uniform with all his medals. Many men are trying to
get enough medals through their work that their earthly
fathers might give them what only the heavenly Father be-
stowed on His Son and His other sons in the faith: "You are my
beloved Son, in whom I am well pleased!" (Mark 1:11; Rom.
8:14–15; Eph. 1:3).

Our early mentors also play an important role in how we
view work. We encounter these men early in our work experience. They teach us how to work; they show us the ropes and
how they think we ought to work. They teach us the rules of
the game. Daniel Levinson says a good mentor is the combination of a good father and a good friend, "a transitional figure
who invites and welcomes a young man into the adult
world. . . . He serves as guide, teacher and sponsor." However,
he also points out that

like all love relationships, the course of a mentor relationship
is rarely smooth and its ending is often painful. . . . There is
plenty of room for exploitation, undercutting, envy, smoth-
ering, and oppressive control. . . . After the relationship has
been terminated, both parties are susceptible to the most
intense feelings of admiration and contempt, appreciation

and resentment, grief, rage, bitterness and relief—just as in the wake of any significant love relationship.[14]

Whether they like us, value our performance, or reject us as not fitting in or being more suited to other work, our mentors' view of us has a profound effect on us for years. Unfortunately, many mentors mentioned to me are of the predator type. These older men perceive younger male workers as threats who must quickly be shown who is going to be boss. They cannibalize the young men's energy, their ideas, and often their products. These bosses give their new recruits the worst jobs to "test" their loyalty and to break the "maverick horse" within them. In the corporate world, a loose cannon cannot be tolerated. Even Lt. Col. Oliver North finally got his!

For young men eager for the praise of their seniors, the predator model becomes deterministic. The young loose cannon at heart finally conforms, suffering the rejection of his mentors and inwardly saying to himself, "I'm going to prove to them and to myself that I can be someone despite all odds and their view of me." Therefore, his movement up the corporate ladder is always sending a message to someone somewhere, or at least he hopes it does.

By the way, research suggests that the victim usually becomes a predator. He uses the reasoning that because something happened to him, he is justified in doing the same to other young upstarts: "If my mentors were tough, I'm going to be tough, too, or outdo them by being tougher!" And we wonder why work is called a jungle!

A few of us have had nurturing mentors. These men could critique the company. They saw beyond the system and stood their ground to nurture what they considered essential, even at the expense of putting people over company policy or at the risk of opposing accepted practice. These mentors loved us, praised us, and taught us what was really important. They knew the rules, but they valued the relationships. If we were fortunate, we were part of such a relationship. But even though we have had nurturing mentors, there can be a downside to the experience. The greatness of the relationship also marks the way a man works for life.

Recently, I recognized how I have been trying to live up to the model of one of my mentors. I don't believe he ever articulated any life expectations for me, but somehow the impact of his life on mine left such an imprint that I have felt the expectation to compare my life to his. He gave me early adult dreams to pursue. However, my life has taken totally different tracks, tracks that compared to his may be viewed as mistakes or failures. I have had to ask myself, Was I trying to be as great as he was? Or was I trying to unconsciously prove to him that I was still a faithful disciple? As much as I value the relationship, I have now reached the point that I see I have to be me, and I will never be what he was or do what he has done. I hope I'm growing up. I'm no longer working to please my mentors or to prove anything to anyone anywhere, except to myself.

Work as the Scriptures Regard It

Before I begin this last section, I must acknowledge my gratitude to the work of Bill Hendricks and Doug Sherman. They have provided in their book *Your Work Matters to God* a needed and carefully thought-out evaluation of work in our society today from a Judeo-Christian point of view. They list the following biblical purposes for working: "Through work we serve people, through work we meet our own needs, through work we meet our family's needs, through work we earn money to give to others, through work we love God."[15]

To get a thorough clarification of each point, read the entire book. My conclusions are similar to those in their work.

The first thing we learn from the Scriptures is that God created man and placed him in the Garden to serve and guard it (Gen. 2:15). Caring for it was man's first responsibility, his first work. As such, work is inherently good and reflects our relationship with the Creator, who is also a worker. Not working is dehumanizing to oneself since God made man in His own image to be a worker.

But when sin entered the world, Adam fell, and so did his work. Work under sin became servitude (Gen. 3:17). After sin entered the world, work involved pain and stress; man had to put more into the labor than what he derived from it. This theological concept is picked up in the Solomonic observations about work. Solomon uses a word for work throughout Ecclesiastes (Hebrew, *'amal*), which means "labor under difficult toil and pain." He calls it "burdensome" (Eccles. 1:13), "vanity and grasping for the wind" (1:14).

Often the perception of work as servitude has been deemed the biblical view—apart from other teachings of Scripture. In the book of Exodus, however, God views the servitude of His people not as healthy but as wrong for them. In the Exodus account, He reaffirms again and again that oppression and bondage to the work of the Egyptians make God's people unable to hear His voice through His spokesman, Moses (3:7; 4:22–23; 5:4–19; 6:9; 8:1; 9:1; 10:3). God Himself says His people need to be free from the servitude of the Egyptians to serve Him. I conclude from this that vocational servitude can reduce one's ability to serve God. Any vocational reductionism is dehumanizing and makes the worker less able to be what God wants him to be. Work should not be servitude, and when it becomes mere servitude, it is a denial of the image of God. Man was not created to be in servitude to men; he is to serve God alone.

The Scriptures underscore this principle. Employers are admonished to treat their employees fairly (Col. 4:1). Slaves are encouraged to seek their freedom if possible (1 Cor. 7:21), and masters are encouraged to view their slaves from the high position of Christian dignity (Philem. 16). The year of Jubilee, based on the Sabbatic year (Lev. 25) demonstrates God's desire that His people not be in perpetual work-related servitude

(Exod. 20:9–11). They must eventually be set free because as God's people they are free beings!

Our problem with work as servitude is that we actually prefer slavery to freedom because it is safer. We would love to be freewheeling entrepreneurs. Some persons even think of themselves as such but never sacrifice the security of their servitude for the freedom of enjoying work or doing what they really want to do. Those who face economic realities of house payments, fees for college education, and debt reduction obviously can't walk out on existing jobs. But at least we can see *why* we are working and realize fully that our vocational servitude can sometimes greatly reduce our ability to serve God.

> *Our problem with work as servitude is that we actually prefer slavery to freedom because it is safer.*

We must weigh the alternatives, make our choices, and gain some control over our lives. I believe that the Scriptures do not place a value on servitude. There is no inherent blessing in being a slave to work itself. Work may be hard, and we may have to make many sacrifices for other reasons, but no magical quality about work makes us more spiritual or significant in the eyes of God because of its existence.

Though the Scriptures have much to say on the subject, work generally seems to be looked upon as a personal responsibility and contribution. The primary responsibility is to oneself and to one's family (2 Thess. 3:10–12; 1 Tim. 5:8). Ignoring this responsibility and becoming totally dependent on others are not in keeping with the spirit of the Bible. However, it is wrong to draw the conclusion that when one is out of work or is not able to make it financially, the person was not working hard enough or had a fatal flaw.

The doctrine of meritocracy runs deep in our culture. It is

easy to write off economic downturns, hostile takeovers, and personnel trimmings as "getting what one deserves." Illustrations abound of firms' firing the best employees while retaining less-competent ones. Many highly paid, competent employees have had security guards "help" them empty out their desks and escort them out the back door. The humiliation accompanying this all-too-frequent reality is incredible. Yet, because it happens doesn't mean it was deserved. Human nature being what it is, we think it probably was deserved when it happens to others, but when we are the victims, we are sure the company was at fault.

The family of faith also has the responsibility to support the concerns of God in the world and in the church. We work so that we might through our financial resources and job opportunities be responsible to support those things that God has revealed in His Word as important to Him. Whether it is sharing Christ with persons who do not know Him, giving to the poor, or helping to raise a church's budget, we are encouraged to work as a part of our personal contribution to God's concerns in the world.

The last area of responsibility and contribution is the one to our larger world. In the final analysis our work is not only for ourselves or for the church but for a larger slice of life. I believe every human at some point in life wrestles with why he or she is in this world. A Jewish friend once commented on the difference between the way he was raised and the way most gentile boys (goyim) are reared. In a goyish home, the mother tells her son as he goes out the door to school in the morning to "be good." The summum bonum of life is being good, which means not getting into trouble. However, my friend recalled his mother's saying, "Do something great today!" His Jewish mother had instilled the aspect of contribution to life. We are here not only for ourselves but also for a larger contribution. Our contributions will probably flow from our unique gifts and talents, and expressing these gifts and talents in and through our work is a worthy aim.

Often today the Christian takes an uncritical approach to employment, as if any job is appropriate for a Christian. Tom Sine charges us to think a little more about our jobs and the contribution they are really capable of making. He says,

> Don't misunderstand me. There is nothing inherently un-Christian about being a carpenter, a businessman, or a factory worker. But as Christians we must ask why we are doing our jobs, what consequences our work will have in our society and our world, and how our work will contribute to the advance of God's Kingdom.[16]

God gave gifted individuals with particular skills for constructing His tabernacle (Exod. 31:1–5, 11) and the Solomonic temple (2 Chron. 2:11–14) and for upbuilding the body of Christ, the church (Eph. 4:7). These skilled individuals were called through their giftedness to larger purposes than making a living for themselves. It is reasonable to assume that since they were skilled, their work reflected a sense of excellence, and their personal benefit was in their feelings of worthwhileness and meaning. They were aware of contributing to something larger than their lives.

The list of biblical characters and the jobs they worked is endless. Almost every profession is there. Each person struggled in the relationship with God and to the world while working at a daily vocation. We can think of Joseph, managing Potiphar's household and later serving as prime minister of Egypt. There are Nehemiah, a cupbearer to a King; Esther, a beauty pageant contestant; Amos, a picker of figs; Joseph and Mary running a carpenter's shop; Aquila and Paul in the tentmaking business together. They all worked, and their work was not always easy. But they apparently saw beyond their work to the ultimate meaning of life. Each made a unique contribution to history, to the community, to the world.

Making a contribution doesn't necessarily involve becoming president of the company or leading a social concern. Often it is mere presence. For many of us, our contribution lies in being the kind of people we are, and that is often overlooked by organizations or groups. Mothers and fathers make contributions to and through their kids. My hope is that this book will be my contribution to you. A contribution takes place any time my life rubs off on someone else. In a world where everyone is working for different reasons, making the whole arena of work uneasy for men, it is comforting to realize that my contribution in work will often be unconscious. I may have the greatest effect when I least expect it.

I remember walking by a Sunday school classroom at church and looking through the door window. I noticed a man on the floor who was the president of a very large Philadelphia company. Four- and five-year-olds were all over him. He had contributed not only to the lives of those kids but also to his pastor that day!

Doug Sherman and Bill Hendricks believe the ideal, though tough to find, is to have a job you love and one you are convinced is worth doing.[17] They assert,

> The main thing in your search for the right job is to deepen your understanding of how God has put you together and how you can make your greatest contribution. . . . In any case, you should regard the job as important but not all-important. It should honor Christ and serve others. But keep in mind the limitations to work. No job can provide total and/or ultimate fulfillment. But if you find a sense of contentment in your work, rejoice! It is the gift of God.[18]

Work is not easy for men or women. The paycheck does not come easy. There are many binds and pressures. Between trying to please bosses, ourselves, and God, the binds sometimes seem insurmountable. Fortunately, no matter how well rewarded we are for the work we do, God sees the heart, and that makes our work a little less difficult. One man's work is another man's devotion. Some men's work is their devotion, and some men's devotion is their work.

Of Abraham Heschel, a Jewish mystic, the story is told:

At a party a guest turned to Heschel, and said, "In the town in Poland I came from, I knew an old Hasid, he would rise at the outlandish hour of 5 o'clock in the morning, make his way to the synagogue, where he would proceed to disturb everyone with his loud, endless prayers and his study, never pausing for breakfast or lunch, until about 5 o'clock in the afternoon when he took nourishment. Now tell me, is that what you call religion? Is that a sensible life for man?" Heschel was pained, but he listened thoughtfully, then replied: "Isn't that strange, I know someone just like that right here in New York. He is almost an exact parallel to that old Hasid. He, too, gets up very early in the morning, devotes himself with singleminded passion to his work, and hardly tastes food during the day until late in the afternoon. Indeed, he worked so hard that at 42 he suffered a stroke! There is only one difference between the two—the purpose of this one's work is money! Now, tell me, is such behavior commensurate with reason or common sense? Yet, you belittle the one and probably admire the other, Why?"

The man's reply: "But that Hasid didn't do anything with his life. Who cared about his prayer and study?" Heschel replied, "Isn't it possible that God cared?"[19]

It's an uneasy paycheck, but God cares! How we earn our living is often made more difficult by having to live alone. If childhood, marriage, friends, and work are not easy, neither is the single life. Male solitude is uneasy as well.

CHAPTER 5

Uneasy Solitude

Or Why Men Remarry So Fast

———— ■ ————

Of all the chapters in this book, this one is probably the most difficult for me to write. It's difficult for the simple reason that I've been married for the last twenty-three years. What do I know about what it's like to be a single adult male? There are many assumptions behind this feeling, the first of which is that married males are never alone or feel alone, and that marriage by itself cures all male needs for companionship. It doesn't. The question also begs the issue that as a man I have forgotten what it was like to be single, or that there is anything to be learned from single men. My married years have not been isolated from single friends, who have spent hours in our home or over dinners sharing intimacies. We, as husband and wife, have learned much from our single friends of both sexes.

Whether men are married or single, we have one thing in common: neither married life nor the single life has been easy. Solitude can be just as uneasy for the male as marriage can. In fact, one researcher suggests that single males are at serious risk in our society. George Gilder, author of the best-seller *Sexual Suicide*, has updated his work and concludes,

> The single man is poor and neurotic. He is disposed to criminality, drugs, and violence. He is irresponsible about his debts, alcoholic, accident-prone, and susceptible to disease. Unless he can marry, he is often destined to a troubled and abbreviated life. . . . And their ranks have been growing. Between 1970 and 1982, the ranks of single men jumped 78% to 19.4 million. . . . In general, men have more psychological problems than women, and single men have the most problems of all. . . . Crime, like poverty, correlates far better with sex and singleness than it does with race. . . . Single males have the highest mortality rate and suicide is increasingly the way they die. In fact, the older a man gets without marrying, the more likely he is to kill himself.[1]

The solution to this problem has been marriage. But marriage by itself is an interesting relationship for men. Marriage has been likened to the situation of flies at the window: those on the inside want out, and those on the outside want in. Singles think the chief end of man is to get married, while many marrieds secretly long to be single again.

The "single" male experience starts early. By single, I mean thinking of yourself as single. Early on, boys think of themselves as boys, not singles. The single handle is of more adult origin, which plays host to much more expectation and meaning than mere boyhood. The concept of singleness automatically puts us into the male-female relationship, whether we want to be there or not. Elementary boys don't think about being single, even when they think about girls. Girls are girls, and boys are boys. You like some girls and hate others. It's all fairly simple and clear. But adulthood fouls up a lot of things.

I remember my first kiss (third grade), but it wasn't until the eighth grade that I *had* to think about where I was with the opposite sex. The well-meaning guidance counselor apparently took it upon himself to check out all the guys to see if their development was "normal." In the context of talking to me about trade school versus high school, he dropped the question out of nowhere, "Have you found the girls?" It seemed humorous, but I dared not laugh. I finally blurted out, "Sure." He replied, "Good." I passed the test!

At the time, I was interested in basketball, my studies, and TV shows. That was about it. I didn't know an "in" group and an "out" group existed in the school. My eyes weren't open yet. I didn't know that two kinds of people were at Robinson Junior High: those who walked in pairs (boys with girls), and those who didn't. I didn't talk on the phone at nights. I did my homework, watched TV, and went to bed to repeat the process the next day.

Then it happened! I really discovered the girls . . . in one girl. Actually, *I* was discovered. A friend told me that someone watching me play basketball thought I was cute and would like to go out with me. I didn't know what "going out" meant, since I didn't know kids met at parties to dance and neck. I was excited and scared all in one big burst of emotion. The next day I saw her in the lunchroom. Wow, how could I have missed such a beauty! I'm sure I had seen her, but the realization that someone likes you changes everything; you see differently. Now some thirty years later, I don't remember how I got up enough courage to break the ice. In typical male fashion, I probably got a friend to do it. But we did get together.

I was quickly placed into the "in" group because I had a girlfriend. My grades went down, I talked on the phone at nights, and I never played the games the same. No matter what the score or how important the game, I always had one eye on the stands. The other eye was usually on the cheerleaders, just in case. After the games, for the school dances, proms, and Friday and Saturday nights, I had a standing date. Lynne and I were a couple. Being a couple gave us an identity with each other during a time when identity was fragile and spurious. We dated through high school and for most of college. Then she married someone else.

Female Security Blankets

> *We as men have a tendency to use women in our relationships as security blankets, which in the long term undermines our development.*

My personal history illustrates how we as single men enter the dating process and discover so much meaning in it, to the point of finding much of our identity in it. It also illustrates how we as men have a tendency to use women in our relationships as security blankets, which in the long term undermines our development. The opposite sex gives us a certain sense of security and significance. There is a tremendous amount of security in being part of a couple and "going steady." In adulthood, the pressure mounts, making the couple-formation experience the norm and needing a wife a healthy attitude. Male solitude is uneasy because we as men are not used to admitting or seeing our deep-seated needs for the security of women. We simultaneously desire and fear being taken care of by women.

Dr. Ken Druck and James Simmons note this has been called the "Grey Flannel Pampers Syndrome":

[One woman said,] "Jack can be so infuriating at times, on the one hand, he is supportive of my career in banking, and yet he still assumes that the shopping, cooking, and cleaning are my responsibilities. Maybe I shouldn't be surprised. I learned long ago that there is a little boy inside every man I've ever known. Even the big, strong, tough men need you to do the smallest things for them. I can always see it coming—Mommy Time."

—— 80 ——

Men for years have tried to project an image of themselves as strong and independent. But women have never been fooled. They know that even the most powerful men are dependent. A woman friend calls this the "Grey Flannel Pampers Syndrome." The mistake most women make has been to assume that the men themselves realize how dependent they are. But few do. Too many relationships end up today with the woman shouting, "You don't want a woman; you want a mother!" This sense of learned helplessness in such critical areas as self-care, parenting, and housekeeping forces many men into an unhealthy dependency upon women.[2]

Male solitude is uneasy because many of us have not grown up sufficiently to see women as partners and persons rather than as mothers and caregivers. I can use their emotions to do my feeling work for me, use their concern as my concern, use their presence to fill the female vacuum left by my mother.

But someone may ask, "Doesn't the Bible say that it is not good for the man to be alone?" Yes, it does, but even this statement must be put into the larger context. The God of creation had created all the animals in two kinds, male and female. As Adam looked at the creational animal kingdom, no mate was found suitable for him. All species were paired except him. If the first command of God was to be fulfilled (Gen. 1:28) in populating the earth with humans, it was fairly obvious that Adam needed a counterpart who was enough like him to populate it with people but enough different that intercourse could be performed. Man could not populate the earth alone! But after the woman arrived on the scene, the man was told to leave father and mother and cleave to his wife.

This was—and is—a revolutionary concept. The wife has most often left her parents to move into the husband's life and family circle. This creational model places priority and importance on the male's leaving (mentally, emotionally, physically) so that he can become one with his wife. The implication is that true intimacy with a woman involves a man's relinquishment of the expectation that she will be a mother (parent) to him. Attaining intimacy means seeing oneself not as a child to be taken care of but as an initiating partner in the relationship. It means being a whole, grown-up person. But growing up is never easy, so our solitude is never easy.

Single Sexuality

One cannot talk long today about male singleness without getting into the subject of single sexuality. For a more in-depth discussion of the subject I recommend Thomas F. Jones's book *Sex and Love When You're Single Again,* also published by Oliver-Nelson. For my purposes here, I would like to discuss two common myths I have recognized about single sexuality in men.

The first myth is that all single men must be sexually active. From our culture, it would appear that a single man who is not interested in or involved in a sexual experience is either a liar or not a "real" man. The common locker-room consensus is very much the same as Zorba the Greek's when he tells the young man, "Never refuse a woman who wants to go to bed with you; you are not a man if you do." I can't quote national statistics on the subject, but I have been very surprised and pleased by the numbers of single men who have confided in me. What has impressed me the most is their concern for this area of life. Even in their struggles and failures, there is a common theme; at least some men who are responsible in their jobs and competent in their personal associations do not believe they need sex to have a meaningful relationship with the opposite sex. Whether they believe premarital sex is wrong or not, they confirm to me that not everyone is sexually active or has to be sexually active to really be a man.

The myth makes single manhood difficult, but some are victorious and many more want to be. Single Christian men need to be reminded that some of the greatest thinkers and saints of the church—such as Augustine, Anselm, and Thomas Aquinas—have been sexual celibates. More recently, Malcolm Muggeridge and C. S. Lewis remained celibate after the deaths of their wives. Their achievement says to me that purity is possible, a fact that needs to be proclaimed from the housetops, especially in our permissive, AIDS-infected society.

The second myth is that men can never be friends with women. The relationship will eventually become romantic and thus sexual, or the friendship will end altogether. In other words, single men (or married ones) really don't want nonromantic relationships. They stay in a relationship because of a romantic or sexual attraction, no matter what they may say. In the world of male Christianity, does a man want to have a brother-to-sister relationship with a woman, or is there always another agenda, no matter how unconscious it may be?

This myth is hard to either confirm or deny. I'm even hard-pressed to call it a myth, but I believe it is—not necessarily because there's enough research to prove it, but because I see so much of it confusing the dating relationship on both sides. In this regard, I will make a point that will anger some of my women readers, especially the single ones. I think this myth is perpetuated and believed by many single women, even when it is not practiced or believed by men. It surfaces in the relationship under the heading of commitment. A standing joke told by female singles in a particular singles' ministry is this: "Do you know how single women in this church get rid of the bugs in their kitchen? Ask for a commitment!"

Feeding this myth is the desire of single women for commitment from the single men they date. Don't read me wrong, I believe in defining relationships and letting a person know where you stand. However, in the adult single dating relationship, there is an agenda. If the male myth is sexual, the female myth is commitment. In reality, the female cannot be friends with a male without becoming or wanting to become romantic. After some time in the relationship, the woman begins to push for commitment from the single man. The fault is not totally hers; a single man can lead a woman along a path that makes her think it is going to lead to marriage and then drop her with the I-just-want-to-be-friends response. I don't encourage that at all, but I do see the myth perpetuated by the hopes and dreams a woman has in every possible candidate for marriage.

From the beginning of the relationship, the man may enjoy the friendship aspects but know that the relationship should not move toward something more. When he feels the pressure to make a commitment, he flees, only proving to himself that he can't really have a friendship with a woman; it must lead to something romantic. For the female in the relationship, his actions confirm the myth that men can't commit.

I would like to believe there are many reasons why a man can't make a commitment to a woman. Sometimes, he feels very comfortable with a woman, enjoys her company, and shares many common interests, but there is no "magic." The most common question singles ask me has to do with this magic: What do I do if there is no "magic"? What is this magic? I have no idea, but I know if it is there or not. Does one marry and commit simply because there is magic? Absolutely not! Does one marry if there is no magic? I wouldn't recommend it. I've seen too much magic fade with time; however, I would caution against marrying out of pure logical, cold appraisal of the relationship. Women must accept the fact that sometimes there's magic and sometimes there's not.

Men also have the inability to trust, which gets transferred to the realm of commitment. Because of parental dysfunction or past personal hurts from other relationships, often men protect themselves in their relationships and are not about to bestow the greatest trust in their lives—trusting another human being to be what they appear to be. Men who have problems trusting usually need specialized counseling to identify the unresolved hurts affecting their present relationships.

Singles aren't the only ones who have problems with commitment. It's part and parcel of our cultural environment. Where does anyone see true commitment today? Am I committed to my job? No, not really; only until a better one comes along. How about my choice of restaurants, food, cars, and toothpaste? No, we realize it is pointless to be faithful or committed to such things when in a few years the food will no longer be consistently good, the car will break down, or the company will be taken over by foreign investors. Radio stations have to offer clever money giveaways or free tickets to keep their audiences tuned to them. Everyone knows that people are spinning the dial all day long unless there's some reward for listening. As soon as they win, they get really committed. The announcer asks, "Who plays more oldies and gives away more money every hour?" The answer with fervency comes, "ZIP 100!" But as soon as they pick up their check, their commitment goes out the window.

> *Here is a sociological reality. In a pluralistic society where a multitude of choices exists, commitment is difficult.*

Here is a sociological reality. In a pluralistic society where a multitude of choices exists, commitment is difficult. For single men, it makes their manhood uneasy. Why is it difficult? Let me offer a simple illustration in answer to that. Several years ago, I taught in Bolivia during a summer. Since I enjoy very rich South American coffee, I wanted to bring some back with me to enjoy in the States. I took a little walk to the Cochabamba market. I asked for four kilos of coffee and was given four kilos of coffee. Simple. Later that same year, at Thanksgiving several relatives and guests came over. Cinny, my wife, asked me to find an open grocery store because we had run out of coffee. I found a store, went in, and stood looking up and down the coffee aisle for many minutes. The Bolivian experience returned to my mind, and I started laughing. As I looked at the long aisle with what seemed like hundreds of kinds of coffee, I found myself making no decision at all for fear of making the wrong decision. Cinny hadn't told me what kind of coffee to get: freeze dried, drip, perk, decaf? That's what happens in a society like ours. America is the land of choices for any product, including who to date and marry, and we don't want to make any mistakes.

I genuinely respect many of my single adult friends of both genders for their lack of commitment. If I was a single person in my thirties or forties, having never married or having gone through a divorce, I would be especially careful about who I would commit my life to. Given the current divorce rate and the number of unhappy marriage partners who stay together, marriage is nothing to jump into. However, the stats for men suggest they marry faster every year, especially after coming out of one relationship or marriage. This tendency may reflect their need for mother that they may not have come to terms with.

One other related reason for men's lack of commitment is that sometimes they fear the unknown, which is complicated by a lack of faith. I've counseled several single men through their courtships; they really do want to commit, but they continue to hold back. They just don't want to take the plunge. They are like the sprinter Harold Abrahams in the movie *Chariots of Fire*. Having lost his first race, he wants to quit and tells his girlfriend, "If I can't win, I don't want to run." She wisely counters, "You can't win if you don't run."

All good things require risk. Marriage *is* a risk, but sometimes single males need someone to push the risk a little. I've done this on a couple of occasions. After several sessions with a couple in premarital counseling, I have determined they know each other well enough and there has been sufficient time for the relationship to normalize. I tell them, "I will give you two weeks to determine whether to marry or not. If you decide not to marry, will you agree to go your separate ways, cultivate other relationships, and not communicate with each other again?" I don't recommend this as an absolute principle, but when I sense everything else is right in the relationship, I conclude they need a little push to make the decision. All of us marry by faith without any real guarantee of the outcome.

But so much for the mythology surrounding this frustrating experience of being part of a couple. I really want to address the goals of adult singleness.

Purposes for Single Adulthood

Despite all the changes brought about by the sexual revolution in the sixties, I see very little change in the way the public at large views adult singles. From concerned mothers to business partners to pastors, the single male is often looked upon as suspect, an anomaly, a nonfunctional being. Some may even ponder if he has gay tendencies. The assumption is fundamental: the goal of the adult single life is marriage. If one is not married after some time (usually age thirty), people begin to wonder what is wrong. Therefore, I challenge the assumption.

> *From concerned mothers to business partners to pastors, the single male is often looked upon as suspect, an anomaly, a nonfunctional being.*

Is the ultimate purpose in the adult single's life to find a spouse? I believe not! That is comparable to saying the goal of adult married life is to please one's spouse and meet all her needs. I believe we are thinking too narrowly here about life for both married and single persons. Associating life goals with only one relationship places extreme pressure on that relationship, probably more pressure than the relationship can stand. Besides, I don't believe God looks at the world in two categories, married and single. This issue is a cultural thing. The very book that records where the institution of marriage came from (Gen. 2) also has much to say about our individual purposes, whether married or single.

Contentment

Biblical scholars argue among themselves over whether they think the apostle Paul was married, whether his wife died (if he had one), or whether he obtained a divorce for the sake of the kingdom. But they all agree on one thing; he is single when he writes his letters. He writes as a single man with apparently little interest in marriage (1 Cor. 7:8). He realizes its importance (Eph. 5:22–33) and tries to regulate it in God-honoring ways, but for him personally, his purposes and goals are elsewhere.

For regulating any believer's life, male or female, he underscores the attribute of contentment. In one letter he says, "Be anxious for nothing. . . . For in whatever state I am, I have learned to be content" (Phil. 4:6, 11). He says that even godliness without contentment is worthless (1 Tim. 6:6), and that he had learned to be content with his weaknesses (2 Cor. 12:10).

I do not see this Paul as a passive, accepting-whatever-happens wimp. He knew where he wanted to go (Rom. 15:24) and was ambitious for the ministry God had given him (Phil. 1:12). I don't believe Paul copped out on life. He had drive, for there was much to be accomplished, but at the same time he valued contentment. It almost appears that he knew full well how much the change of major life stations would disrupt one's inner contentment. Therefore, he recommended a serious appraisal of one's life before jumping into new relationships.

He wrote,

> Are you bound to a wife? Do not seek to be loosed. Are you loosed from a wife? Do not seek a wife. But even if you

do marry, you have not sinned. . . . But I want you to be without care. He who is unmarried cares for the things of the Lord. . . . But he who is married cares about the things of the world—how he may please his wife (1 Cor. 7:27–33).

He said this even though he encouraged younger women to marry and have children (1 Tim. 5:14). Apparently, Paul was a genuine realist; he knew that the older one gets, the more difficult it is to accept change. It is easier to make significant life changes when one is young. But the overarching principle is contentment, not marriage.

I have seen this tension develop in several individuals, both male and female. One was a Dallas sales rep. He had been dating a girl for over two years off and on, but his travel schedule was always a complicating factor in their relationship. She wanted roots; he was fairly content with his life. He finally asked me, "Is my contentment wrong? I love and care about Susie, but I really like my life right now." I replied, "Does the apostle Paul say contentment is wrong? No, of course not. The only thing you need to determine is whether this contentment is for the right reasons. And do you want to give up this inner satisfaction with your life for the sake of marriage?"

Over the last twenty years in the ministry I've come to two conclusions. First, a lot of singles should surely be married, and second, a lot of marrieds would have been better off staying single. I wish I had the gift of determining the "shoulds" on both ends. But I agree with Paul. Change-of-life relationships can take away much of the basic contentment that singles sometimes take for granted. Contentment is a rare commodity in a stressed-out world. If one is genuinely content with life, even though there are desires for marriage, that contentment must not be minimized. It is a fundamental purpose of single life or married life. The truly contented person is rare.

Enjoyment

In the early fifties, social scientists were concerned that all the new labor-saving devices flooding the market would eventually create a five-hour workday and workweek of three days. Their concern focused on how people would use all their free time. From the perspective of the nineties with less-than-five-year-old laptop computers, cellulars, CD's, and faxes, it would seem these inventions have only speeded up our lives and in some mysterious way have produced the opposite effect from what was once projected. Life today is fast-lane for almost everyone I know, even when it is bumper to bumper (which it usually is). New York City friends tell me that on Manhattan, they call it the laser lane! I have to wonder if anyone is really enjoying life.

I tell my single adult friends to enjoy life. Life will never be as simple as when you have only yourself to take care of. That's what I think Paul was trying to communicate to singles. For him, singleness was a time to cultivate undistracted devotion to the Lord apart from the natural distractions that marriage fosters (1 Cor. 7:35). But I believe it goes further than just having less distractions in life. Adults must learn to enjoy life; it is a God-given purpose of human existence.

I can anticipate the response to that statement from some Christians. Enjoying life seems contradictory to giving up yourself and denying yourself for the sake of the gospel teaching. I am convinced the Bible teaches both concepts. As people concerned about the person of Christ, we must always be willing to sacrifice and give ourselves up for others. But does that mean I am *never* to give a thought to myself or seek to enjoy my life? I doubt it.

Paul told one of his young pastors to look seriously to his own life (1 Tim. 4:16), and in the context of telling his readers to look out for the interests of others, he acknowledged that it is normal to look out for one's own interests (Phil. 2:4). Much of what is passed on as good theology and discipleship is sometimes just a subtle form of Gnostic asceticism that does nothing but breed a certain amount of self-abuse.

It is not wrong to enjoy oneself. In fact, the Wisdom Literature of the Bible addresses this theme consistently. It even says a fundamental purpose for a young man is to cultivate joy during his early adulthood. Wise King Solomon writes,

> But if a man lives many years
> And rejoices in them all,
> Yet let him remember the days of darkness,
> For they will be many. . . .
> Rejoice, O young man, in your youth,
> And let your heart cheer you in the days of your youth;
> Walk in the ways of your heart,
> And in the sight of your eyes (Eccles. 11:8–9).

This almost sounds like heresy for those raised with fairly strict religious values asserting that you don't follow your desires because you can't trust them. Others in an attempt to discredit Solomon say, "Yes, but they sure got him in trouble, or he was in some kind of mid-life crisis at that point in his life." But Solomon gives his reason for encouraging young men to enjoy life. He says, "Remove vexation from your heart and put away pain from your body, because childhood and the prime of life are fleeting" (Eccles. 11:10, NASB).

Wow, what a realist! As I write this last line, I can look at myself in the mirror and see the effects of life on my face, hair, and midsection; I've got wrinkles and bald spots, and I've had to make new holes in my belts. I've passed the young man's prime of life. (I'm not exactly sure where it was, but I know I've passed it.) The message is clear from Solomon: you had better enjoy life while you can because eventually the effects of age catch up with you. This message doesn't fly well in an age-denying culture. Even though face-lifts and tummy tucks can help for a while, eventually deterioration sets in, the energy runs out, and one must face the fact that the prime of life has passed. Single men need to realize this. Being single gives tremendous freedom to enjoy life and do many things married men cannot do. I'm not talking about hitting the singles' bars or having multiple sexual encounters. Unfortunately, that's the widely portrayed picture of single men.

A single man in his midtwenties had a fairly good job for being right out of college, and he was dating a girl but was not really serious about her. His parents sent him to see me because they thought he was having an early mid-life crisis. He wanted to quit his job and spend the summer months hitch-hiking around Europe. What would you have told him?

I read the passage in Ecclesiastes about enjoying life and following your desires and also read this admonition: "But know that for all these God will bring you into judgment" (Eccles. 11:9). I told him that it would never be easier to pick up and go and probably come back and find some other work. But when you are forty or fifty, it gets more complicated, if not impossible. If you want to do it, do it now, but remember you don't run away from God when you do. He never went. I don't know why. But at least one person gave him the freedom to go and allowed him to see that it was not contrary to his faith and his personal desires.

I know another young man who did go. He took a year off from graduate school to work for an American company in Saudia Arabia, just for the experience. When he came back, he met a young woman and married.

I do not consider these desires and dreams contradictory to self-sacrifice. I look upon them as very maturing experiences; to have had them is to truly have enjoyed a gift. From all his observations about life, Solomon declares that enjoyment is one of the few things essentially good and beautiful: "It is good and fitting for one to eat and drink, and to enjoy the good of all his labor in which he toils under the sun all the days of his life which God gives him; for it is his heritage" (Eccles. 5:18).

Paul basically repeats the point: "God . . . gives us richly all things to enjoy" (1 Tim. 6:17). Enjoying life and what God has allowed us to have is not wrong; it is good. It might be sinful *not* to enjoy the things God has given us.

Single men, don't let life pass you by while you spend your time looking for a wife. What are your desires, your dreams, your ambitions? What do you enjoy doing? Do those things. You are not getting any younger.

> *What are your desires, your dreams, your ambitions? What do you enjoy doing? Do those things. You are not getting any younger.*

I can't write on this subject without thinking of a good family friend. Tom is single and in his forties; he has grown children from a dissolved marriage. He has played the stocks-and-bonds game, built and sold speedboats, and sold insurance. He installs carpet as a self-employed person. He is the business! Why? So he can set his own schedule, work as much or as little as he desires, and slip off to the Chesapeake whenever he wants and open up his seagoing racer. He knows what he enjoys: people, his boat, and the Lord. He is a beautiful reflection of what the adult single life can be. His enjoyment of life spills over to our home as well. He has the courage to say no to the rat race and so many of the standard upper-middle-class values and not feel guilty about what he enjoys. Thanks, Tom!

Contribution

One of my most severe concerns for marrieds and singles is that we don't wrestle enough with the meaning of our lives. I'm entering a deep well here, but I've noticed that singles tend to look to marriage as a box that must be checked before they can launch out with their life dreams.

Again, the apostle Paul is a premier model of the single male adult life. I believe he thought and lived his life in terms of contribution. When he looked at his life (having been transformed by a personal confrontation with the living Messiah), he realized that his life was a stewardship. Life is to be enjoyed and to have its contentments, but it is also to have its contribution. Paul labored on the bases of purpose and life meaning

(Col. 1:28–29). He sought to make a contribution to the kingdom of God through his life (1 Thess. 2:11–12), and he knew at the end of his life he had accomplished something (2 Tim. 4:7–8) toward that purpose.

Often singles are so busy establishing careers and looking for spouses that they don't deal with the big question of life: Why are we here? That question is not something merely to be studied in a meaning of existence course in college or as part of a philosophy course. It is the quest that both believers and unbelievers must sooner or later face.

For Viktor Frankl, it took being a Jewish psychiatrist at Auschwitz to finally and fully face the meaning of life. He writes,

> I doubt whether a doctor can answer this question in general terms. For the meaning of life differs from man to man, from day to day and from hour to hour. What matters, therefore, is not the meaning of life in general but rather the specific meaning of a person's life, at a given moment. . . . One should not search for an abstract meaning of life. Everyone has his own specific vocation or mission in life to carry out a concrete assignment which demands fulfillment. Therein, he cannot be replaced, nor can his life be repeated. Thus, everyone's task is as unique as is his specific opportunity to implement it. As each situation in life represents a challenge to man and presents a problem for him to solve, the question of the meaning of life may actually be reversed. Ultimately, man should not ask what the meaning of life is, but rather he must recognize that it is *he* who is asked. In a word, each man is questioned by life: and he can only answer to life by answering for his own life; to life he can only respond by being responsible.[3]

Too often single men fail to ponder what talents, experiences, and contributions they can give to life. In a sense, they are waiting for things to happen to them and for them and not recognizing that God has created them in His own image. As creative expressions of the living God, they can make unique contributions. Marrieds may share this mere waiting and functioning malaise. But I bring up this subject because singles are sometimes freer to think about contribution. Frankl and others have linked enjoying good mental health to being an involved individual, contributing to society, to the needs of others, and to the church. Also, this sense of purpose is critical to one's survival during extreme stress and trauma.

In American culture we have bowed before the shrine of individualism, and perhaps today we are paying the price of everybody's doing his own thing. It is time to think in terms of purposes larger than the individual and individual fulfillment.

In my church single adults have done many things that put the marrieds to shame. From going on mission trips to taking meals to the poor, the single adults in our church demonstrate repeatedly that singles are not selfish yuppies merely concerned about their foreign cars and cellular phones. They are caring, sacrificing, and contributing individuals.

A real tragedy is to see single men turned in on themselves. As Billy Graham once said, "The smallest package in the world is a human being all wrapped up in himself." I have seen an amazing cycle take place. I have met single men who think they have severe problems, and some seek counselors. Often the counseling makes them more introspective, which confirms that they have problems, which confirms that they need help. I'm sure the Saint Augustines of the world, if they had thought about it long enough, would have found all kinds of mother hatred, unresolved conflicts from their adolescence, and many codependencies. Perhaps if the mental health profession had existed then, *The City of God* would have never been written, and the history of theology would have been much different.[4]

We have stewardship of our lives, and all of us will stand and give an account for what we have done with them. I believe this. Even if I didn't believe it, I think I would probably want to look back on my life when I'm about to die and ask, Did my life make any difference at all to anyone, including my God?

Single Men and the Church

Now I want to discuss how some church traditions regard single men. In some cases, the single male experience is the same experience women have had to face in many areas in their lives. That is, much lip service is given to single males about being equals in the kingdom of God, but when it is time for leadership selection, there exists—or seems to exist—an intrinsic bias toward marrieds. The suspect-single-male problem strikes again.

I've seen it in two areas. The first is the professional staff minister. Try being a single adult minister today, and the vocation options are few or limited. Oh, most churches probably won't admit they favored Marvin Married over Stuart Single because of marital status, but the issue is always there. I know one seminary classmate who recently was a candidate for a staff position. In his early forties and never married, he was never really given serious consideration, although he was qualified for the job. Some feared he might play around too much with other singles in the church. There's also the unarticulated suspicion that he might be gay. The single male at top leadership levels in the church is suspect.

The second area affected by this bias is lay leadership. Single men in the stricter fundamental traditions have faced almost impossible barriers to becoming elders or deacons. Church boards are almost always made up of marrieds. It's ironic to see churches that pride themselves on having representative leadership on their boards but have only married men on the boards, even when women and single men have very high percentages in the congregation.

These attitudes communicate to single men that they are not yet grown up; they are not deemed adults. Let's face it. In

> *Let's face it. In many churches, the real rite of passage into adulthood is marriage. If you haven't been through the experience, you aren't considered an adult.*

many churches, the real rite of passage into adulthood is marriage. If you haven't been through the experience, you aren't considered an adult. One church I know is probably more willing to place a divorced single on its board than a never-married single. Being male and single in the church is just another area where manhood is uneasy.

Unplanned Solitude

The solitude that comes to a man as the result of events often beyond his control is not easy. In growing proportions men find themselves in solitude following divorce or death. These men had not planned on being or living alone, but suddenly or gradually they are on the outside of marital life. They are single, but they are a different kind of single. They have a common bond that makes their maleness different from that of other men. They have suffered loss and must adjust to new and different living situations, single parenthood, and an overall feeling that life has lost its taste.

Whether the loss of a spouse occurred through death or divorce, the result for the male is the same: he is alone again. And most men don't take this aloneness well.

George Gilder graphically alludes to this wounded male:

Perhaps the most dramatic evidence of the literally vital importance of the marriage tie to men is the impact of its rupture by divorce and widowhood. Contrary to the usual images of the helpless and abandoned wife, the statistics show far greater evidence of helpless and traumatized husbands. . . . But in terms of mental and physical disease and life expectancy, divorce damages the man far more than the woman. Thus, divorced men are more likely to seek psychiatric help than divorced and separated women and they can be found in disproportionate numbers in mental hospitals. They are also more prone to profess unhappiness than divorced women . . . In addition, the impact of marriage on character is not merely a statistical conclusion. One does not have to look far to find examples of buccaneer singles transformed by marriage or to find examples of once-stable men plunged into depression and drink by widowhood or divorce.[5]

One man, who filed for his divorce, told me he didn't understand his feelings: "Why do I feel so much loss when I wanted to be alone and single?" He is a fairly typical out-of-touch-with-his-feelings male. I answered, "We men sometimes merely look at marriage like we do joining a club or an organization. We sign on the dotted line, pledge ourselves to the rules of the organization, and that's that. Then if something happens that we don't like, we simply pull our membership and go elsewhere. Simple. No emotion involved. We assume marriage is the same way." I then added, "But losing a spouse is not like pulling your membership. It's like losing a limb. Even when a man has a cancerous limb and wants to get rid of it to save his life, he will feel a tremendous sense of loss. A wife is part of yourself, your history, your time, your money, your kids. This person doesn't merely walk out of your life, and you quickly move on as if nothing happened." Oh, some men try to deny that they feel anything, but sooner or later it comes out.

Following the Delta L1011 crash at the Dallas–Ft. Worth International Airport, my services were required. One man talked to me a few days after being told his ex-wife had been killed. I asked him, "Is there anything you wish you could have told her?" He started to cry, "I wish I could have told her that life with her wasn't as bad as I made her think it was." He had divorced her and wanted her out of his life, but much was buried with her. A lot of his own history and shared experience went down with her, never to be regained.

An interesting phenomenon with men is their speedy formation of new relationships with women. J. Eugene Knott observes, "Compared to widows, widowers seem to reattach to new women in relationships more often and sooner."[6] It is as if they so view themselves as married men—or a man in relation to a woman—that facing their aloneness again is too much of a shock. The Grey Flannel Pampers Syndrome may be rearing its ugly head again. Men can't perceive being without a mother figure in their lives caring for them. Therefore, they move very quickly into new relationships and remarry at incredible rates.

I asked a family sociologist about the statistics on how rapidly widowed men remarried after the deaths of their wives. He answered, "Let me put it this way. At the funeral they are probably looking around for the most eligible single female who more often than not is one of the wife's best friends from old."

Unplanned solitude is not easy for men. They try to fill the pain of the broken relationship with another relationship and in the process may miss some of life's biggest lessons, lessons about who they really are as men. Fresh Start, an international divorce-recovery seminar, suggests that a divorced person not seek a serious relationship for at least two years after a marriage has ended. The simple reason is that it usually takes a minimum of two years to work through the normal emotions experienced as a result of divorce. Anger, depression, denial, and bargaining with God—all can get mixed with the romantic intensity of a new relationship. If infatuation strikes hard on the never-married, it acutely hits the newly divorced and widowed. One man I know remarried so soon after the death of his wife that his grown kids couldn't cope with it, and they wanted almost nothing to do with him.

In *Second Chances*, Judith Wallerstein and Sandra Blakeslee reveal that the divorce recovery experience in particular has unique tasks:

The danger in every crisis is that people will remain in the same place, continuing through the years to react to the initial impact as if it had just struck. The opportunities in every crisis are for people to rebuild what was destroyed or to create a reasonable substitute; to be able to grow emotionally, establish new competence and pride; and to strengthen intimate relationships far beyond earlier capacities.[7]

Some tasks Wallerstein and Blakeslee list are mourning the loss, reclaiming oneself, resolving or containing passions, venturing forth again, rebuilding, and helping children (if they are present). The authors conclude,

This is the central psychological and social task of divorce, involving all the foregoing tasks as building blocks. The goal is to create a new, sustained adult relationship that will be better than the one left behind and that will include the children or to establish a gratifying life outside of marriage that includes but does not overburden the children. In finding postdivorce stability, a person must allow the obligations, the memories, and the lessons of the past to coexist peacefully with experiences in the present. This is the true essence of second chances. Although I have spelled out these tasks in sequence, each person necessarily goes back and forth, working on one and then another, or on some simultaneously, over the years. Like all else in life, solutions are relative. I have found that some people forgive and most never forget, nor need they. But it is true that new growth can take root only in prepared soil that is not already overgrown. Similarly, new relationships need space created by a person's detaching from the old and being receptive to the new.[8]

After a divorce or the death of a spouse, a man needs understanding and a mourning partner who can walk through his emotions or nonemotion feelings with him. This person should be someone he trusts. I don't believe this person should be of the opposite sex, even though many men have tried to persuade me that a female had filled this role for them. I still see these women as surrogate spouses or mothers, filling the female space left by the wife. However, I'm willing to admit I may be wrong. We are such creatures of denial, often out of touch with our own motives, I'm suspicious of these fast replacements. But I have never been there myself.

Our solitude is not easy. Even our grief work is complicated by our unique male approaches and how it is interpreted by the feminine side.

The solitude men experience is painful and often unseen and misunderstood. Some men come to the conclusion that the only way to deal adequately with what they feel is to marry to fix the pain. Whether conscious or unconscious, the sex motive is probably somewhere in the decision. After all, didn't the apostle Paul say that it is better to marry than to burn? But marriage doesn't make this area of life any easier. Even married sexuality is uneasy!

CHAPTER 6

Uneasy Bedrooms

Or What Men Joke About but Never Really Talk About

———■———

When men begin to talk about the subject of sex, one discovers an entire mythology or at least many misconceptions concerning their sexuality. As I have listened to men and been a coconfessor with them I have become aware of a common experience. There seems to be a basic similarity among the inner lives of men. Their struggles, fears, and misconceptions are mine, too. What we encounter in each other is the sexual beings that we are. When the lid is finally pried off, the inner sexual life is found to be a strange contradiction of beliefs, binds, and often self-destructive behaviors. The distance between what men want and what they get or what they think they should want versus what they end up getting is extreme and sometimes ludicrous.

Over the years as a pastor and counselor, I have reached three conclusions about men's sexuality. First, single men talk

> **Most men believe if they fully revealed the truth about their sexuality, one would think they were either perverted or sexually dysfunctional.**

about and feel guilty about much more than they practice or reveal. Second, married men are probably less sexually active than they are willing to reveal to other men. And third, most men reveal only a small layer (usually the acceptable layer) of their actual sexual experience. Most men believe if they fully revealed the truth about their sexuality, one would think they were either perverted or sexually dysfunctional. That does not leave a lot of middle ground. Dr. Bernie Zilbergeld comments,

> One of the cornerstones of the masculine stereotype in our society is that a man is one who has no doubts, questions, or confusion about sex, and that a real man knows how to have good sex and does so frequently. For a man to ask a question about sex, thereby revealing ignorance, or to express concern, or to admit to a problem is to risk being thought something less than a man.[1]

Even though men may brag about sexual exploits or never say a word about sexuality, our time in the bedroom is not easy. What happens when the bedroom door closes is not necessarily a comfortable expression of love or lust. Uneasy manhood makes our love lives uneasy. Our sex lives reveal as much about who we are as any other area of our lives. But there is the added tension that this subject is very secretive. One source asserts, "The male organization teaches young men that sex is secret, morally wrong, and pleasurable."[2] This statement is even more true for the sons of the faith called Christians. To talk about sex and reveal our stumbling and problems is to be viewed as either unspiritual or sinful. However, to understand the uneasiness of this subject, we must be willing to pierce the pseudospiritual veil and face our deepest motives and fears. Herb Goldberg observes,

> The deepest truths of our psychological makeup are revealed through our sexual response, what turns us on and off, and distance elements that are an expression of the externalized male and the internalized female and express themselves sexually. He moves relentlessly toward disconnection; she moves relentlessly toward fusion (closeness). What turns us on and shuts us down tells us painful truths about our deepest polarized defenses. And then there is much to be learned from our sexual choices and fantasies and the way that these choices play themselves out in our sexual responses.[3]

Facing the realities of our sexual experience may be one of the most spiritually maturing exercises. We find out who we really are and how deeply our convictions, values, motivations, and past experiences affect us. These are deep-seated identity issues for men, and in this area the male ego is very fragile. Whether right or wrong, fiction or fact, adequate sexual functioning is considered proof of masculinity, so any sexual difficulties inevitably damage the male identity.[4] It is hard for us to articulate how we feel about our sexual expressions.

As explained earlier, men do not possess the same kind of self-talk that comes so easily for women, especially the self-talk that focuses on feelings. Herb Goldberg believes the sexes are so polarized by conditioning that it is largely impossible to get "real" men to relate at the feeling level. He describes this bind:

> The deeper psychological reality for men and masculinity is that relating in personal ways is unconsciously threatening, frustrating, and unsatisfying, and in the polarized male/female relationship and within the traditional family dynamic a man can't be different by a simple act of will, even if he wanted, which most men do. . . . The masculine conditioning externalizes and disconnects him, making the

personal side of his life one that is fraught with anxiety and discomfort, while whenever he focuses on impersonal objects, goals, and abstractions outside of himself, he experiences an anxiety reduction, satisfaction, and sense of being a man. . . . In other words, the more masculine he is, the less he can relate personally, regardless of whether or not he wants to.[5]

This reality is not understood widely by either sex. Men probably have a much more realistic idea about feminine sexuality due to the emphasis on it in the feminist movement and feminine psychology writings than women have about men. Because men do not expose their inner selves, especially about sex, to women, many wives and women friends have no idea about the male sexual inner psyche. Consequently, they have many humorous ideas about what male sexuality is all about. When I speak to women's groups on the subject, I find women very surprised. I share new insights concerning male sexuality with them. When one-half of the marital relationship is operating on a different set of assumptions in the bedroom, it is no wonder the bedroom becomes uneasy. The bedroom must be demythologized and rid of these false assumptions. These assumptions are demons that destroy the joyful mutual expression of shared sexuality. Both men and women are harassed by them nightly through their unconscious presence in attitudes and responses.

What are some myths that we allow to cloud our thinking and make our bedrooms uneasy?

Common Male Sexual Myths

Men Want Sex All the Time

The first male myth is that men want sex all the time. I don't know who first started the myth, but it is alive and well. Women really do think that men want sex all the time. Based on my conversations with men, my study of the available research, and my own life, I know men are not this way. However, women again have an advantage. Because of the popular literature and the knowledge that there are times of the month when women are not as sexually motivated, men have grown accustomed to the women's no. A woman can have a headache, or she can be in her time of the month, and these are legitimate noes for a man to accept. The man who questions them or rejects them is insensitive and forces sex upon a woman.

However, a man's saying no to his wife raises questions with other men (who think men should never say no if they are real men) and with his wife. She runs through an entire set of unrelated hypothetical reasons about why he is "really" saying no. She thinks, *Is he having an affair? Am I not attractive to him? Does he really love me? Does he like my best friend better? Is he impotent? Has he lost his job? Does he have AIDS?* All of her questions are based on the myth that men always want sex. If her man doesn't want her at that moment, something must be seriously wrong with either her or him. The simple fact may be that he is tired or he doesn't feel like sex at that moment, no more or less.

It would be nice if women could accept the fact that men sometimes don't feel romantic. It would be exceptional if they would also accept the fact that the momentary feeling does not mean men do not love their wives or that there is anything wrong in the relationship. Men are not sexual machines who must have sex or die. It is important, but not all-important.

> *It would be nice if women could accept the fact that men sometimes don't feel romantic.*

This myth often leads men into another area of a performance-driven relationship. If a man thinks his wife has this view of sex, and his male ego is on the line with reference to her, he often performs the routine to confirm to her that men do want it all the time and he is very much a man, even though he would rather go to sleep. This reasoning is easier and safer than facing his feelings directly, challenging his wife's sexual overtures, and possibly having to discuss "what's wrong with us." The myth has taken a beautiful experience and turned it into merely performing for each other rather than truly relating to each other out of mutual understanding.

Men Need Sex to Relieve Pressure

The second myth runs something like this: men need sex to relieve pressure. I'm sure this one is a carryover from some high-school sex education class or Biology 101 in college. It is based on the facts of semen accumulation in the testicles, which may or may not cause some pain or pressure.[6] However, the facts of the case are probably grossly overexaggerated by some women. Though the wife's intent may be sincere and she genuinely thinks she is meeting her husband's needs by relieving this pressure, in my estimation the argument makes the sexual expression mere servicing!

One wife told me, "If my husband doesn't have sexual intercourse at least once a week, he becomes very irritable." If men need only to relieve pressure, the sexual relationship has become something depersonalized and dehumanized, even demasculinized. A man who has just been serviced by his wife does not feel loved or valued for who he is. He feels like something impersonal or animal-like, just having his fluids drained off to make him feel better.

Men do not need sex to relieve pressure. God in His creative handiwork has already taken care of the pressure problem through the natural nocturnal emissions, which will take place if the fluid buildup is too great. Sexual intercourse for men is far more than relief of pressure. A woman who sees herself servicing her husband's needs has a poor view of sex and an inaccurate understanding of her husband's sexual needs.

A Man Is Satisfied Only When He Climaxes

The third myth is that a man is satisfied only when he climaxes. This makes the final reality the only important reality. If there is no orgasm for a man, sex is meaningless and unfulfilling. Unfortunately, this myth is rooted deeply in the two pornography industries. Yes, I said two! One for men, which promotes the myth, and one for women, which does the same thing. We are more familiar with the first because it is more obvious, more graphic, and more subject to attack.

The X-rated film, video, and magazine industry is largely a male-oriented and male-consumed business. Women are the bait, but men are the fish. This industry portrays the myth of the explosive male orgasm. Everything moves toward that goal, and the orgasm justifies everything up to that point. Bernie Zilbergeld observes,

> There are no ordinary, run-of-the-mill orgasms in most erotic materials. Every orgasm is explosive, body-wrenching and mind-blowing, and even better than the one before. Needless to say, such is not the way it is in the real world. But many of us take the fantasy as our goal and spare no effort to achieve the ultimate orgasm for ourselves or our partners. Compared to the fantasy, real orgasms can feel rather humdrum.[7]

As women in our society are more exposed to (not a play on words) or aware of the male-oriented pornographic material, the myth of The Orgasm for males becomes paramount. Women believe men are not satisfied unless the explosion takes place, and based on this misunderstanding, women get the explosion over with as soon as possible. An additional myth is created that a woman has fulfilled her obligation by giving her man what he really wanted most and what was most important anyway! The male-oriented pornography industry promotes and glorifies a fantasy view of sex, which makes the male orgasm all-important. But so does the female-oriented pornography. It is just as seductive and far more accepted; in the long run it promotes exactly the same mythology.

The word *pornography* comes from two Greek words: *pornos*, which means "a harlot or prostitute and the sexual activity with such a person"; and *graphe*, which means "writing." The words together take on the meaning of writing about sexual activity with harlots or the more general meaning of any writing that portrays illicit sexual relationships. From the consumer's point of view, it is buying an illicit sexual relationship vicariously. It is buying a sexual fantasy.

From this perspective, I take a controversial view that a form of vicarious sexual fantasy is just as pornographic and just as harmful in the sense that it promotes an inaccurate sexual stereotype. Its consumers are largely women, though in the material the bait is both men and women and the concept of romantic love. Love, as presented in this material, ends in the same explosive orgasm. The mythology is found in the daily doses of the afternoon soaps and the romantic trashy love novels that some women talk about.

These novels and afternoon TV episodes portray a form of pornography. It is pornographic because it portrays illicit sexual fantasies for a price and creates an artificial image of normal sexuality. Women "buy" the concept of romantic love, ending in the explosive kiss or bedroom scene, with the same emotions that men experience when they view X-rated materials. Both deal in sexual fiction and receive a psychosexual charge by vicariously experiencing the forbidden fantasies performed by actors and actresses. They are nothing more than print and visual images conceived by writers and acted out by producers and performers, who are being rewarded financially for playing with our sexual minds.

Many people will not accept the idea that soap operas are just as pornographic as *Debbie Does Dallas*, but I believe they are. The images formed in women's minds about male sexuality are powerfully portrayed in these works. Thinking there is no influence on women's minds is like arguing there is no influence on men's minds by a constant exposure (pun intended) to X-rated videos. Yet, very little is said about the impact of this material on women's view of men and the influence it may have on their view of sex and love in marriage.

Compared to a top-selling romantic novelist like Jackie Collins, D. H. Lawrence is rather tame. Nevertheless, the same unrealistic sexual imagery is present in his work. Who reads Lawrence anyway? We all know the answer: women read Lawrence, Collins, and the rest. What Lawrence depicts in vivid verbal images is exactly the same as what is created on camera for the male audience.

Women like the myth as much as men do. For a woman, the image of being swept off her feet, of being caught up so emotionally that she arrives on a distant shore and becomes something she wasn't before, is powerful stuff. It's as powerful as the perfect climax with a superattractive X-rated starlet for a man. Both support the fantasy of the all-important climax.

The reality is that men can and do enjoy touching, kissing, and caressing without having to perform the ultimate orgasmic gymnastics. There are times when men enjoy bringing their wives to a climax and may not even need or want to have an orgasm themselves. They may enjoy intercourse without an orgasm. One man told me that every time he and his wife have intercourse, if he takes longer than five minutes, his wife says, "What's wrong, honey?" The implication is, there is something wrong with him if he doesn't climax immediately. That inhibits his sheer enjoyment of making love with his wife. She would do well to enjoy his loving her, without watching the clock, and learn to enjoy the touching, caressing, and sense of oneness created by their union. Isn't that what women say they really want anyway? If they really desire the holding and caressing, why do they want to have the man climax as quickly as possible? This is a variation on the theme of sex as servicing a spouse. It is unrealistic and untrue, and it reflects an unfortunate attitude toward male sexuality.

Men Have Affairs Because of Sex

Another male sexual myth is that men have affairs because of sex. In other words, a sexual failure at home is the cause of the affair. This myth also subtly dehumanizes men. It makes men purely sexual beings controlled by sexual urges and drives.

Men are more than sexual beings. When men want sex and only sex, plenty of women in our society are ready to provide sex for a price. These working girls don't want entanglements; they don't want to hear how the man feels about life, his marriage, or the stock market. They are available to give a service and obtain a fee. Why do we think prostitution is so successful? Few men fall in love with prostitutes. It is a simple exchange.

However, men fall in love with their secretaries, clients, business associates, fellow choir members, and best friends' wives. The *why*, I am convinced, has little to do with sex. Sex may usually be involved, but sex is not necessarily the primary reason. The reason goes much deeper. The relationship with the other woman meets some unsatisfied needs in the man's life that the relationship with his wife has not met. I have known men with gorgeous, very sensual wives, but they "stumbled" into an affair. When I asked them about the sexual relationship with their wives, more often than not they responded, "Oh, it was great."

This insight is often both good news and bad news for the wife. Good news in the sense that she does not have to feel guilty about not being a good sexual partner for her husband. Bad news because she must evaluate what else about their relationship may not have been what it should or she must merely accept the hardest reality of all—that it just happened and he truly loves her![8]

In these situations, having an understanding of male psychology is important. Sometimes it is almost humorous and virtually irrational to think of a sexually capable man with a very attractive, sexually inviting wife lying in the same bed next to him. Instead of desiring her, however, his sexual desire is heightened for someone else less attractive and much farther removed. It is not a reasonable equation unless we understand the extent to which a man's manhood is uneasy and his bedroom behavior illogical.

Lusting for images or a distant personality when an attractive and willing woman lies next to him defies animal instincts, which means that his male psyche and inner sexual life are quite complex. This reality makes him a higher being and demands that his wife see him as more than a sexual animal. He has feelings, reactions, needs, sensitivities, and turn-ons and turnoffs; the male is an integrated being. His sexual responses are not disconnected from the rest of his life. When he has an affair with another woman, he has an affair with more than her body. He is a relational being, and the quality of his relationships spills over into all areas of his life.

Women are not the only ones who tolerate sexual myths. Men, in turn, also hold to myths about women's sexuality that make their own sexual functioning more difficult.

Men's Myths About Women

Whether we like it or not, whether we admit it or not, we men marry our mothers. Men emotionally have a lot of "little boy" needs that we bring into marriage looking for mothering. Consequently, we seek out and marry Earth Mothers who can care for us, meet our needs, affirm our egos, and bolster our inner selves.

> *Whether we like it or not, whether we admit it or not, we men marry our mothers.*

This first myth is simply put: she should be my Earth Mother. The little boy left in the man makes him want a woman to be and function as a second mother. This attitude obviously does not end at the bedroom door. It pervades the sexual relationship as well. The wife exists to meet his needs, including his sexual appetites. The mother who wiped his nose, made his lunch, and bandaged his scratches becomes the wife who affirms his manhood by mothering him, both emotionally and sexually.

Gordon Dalbey calls this infantile desire idolatry:

> The world continues to enforce the male instinct that protects this primal maternal dependency upon the women loved. "Can't live without you, Baby!", stated variously, is orthodox among pop song writers and listeners. Indeed, the notion has become so customary that a love partner . . . actually believes that to say this to the woman is a demonstration of love, rather than an infantile abdication of one's life, and thus, pure idolatry.[9]

Herb Goldberg exposes this myth for what it really is—irresponsibility. He writes,

> Men want marriage just as much as women do, but for different motives. They want the mothering. . . . They want to validate their masculinity and their lovability but often they don't want to take responsibility for saying, "I really wanted this relationship." . . . In fact, she is really there to satisfy his needs, his own dependency, his isolation, his desperation, his own desire for control, his own need to make sure that she doesn't go with any other men. . . . That takes a little bit of the responsibility from his shoulders.[10]

Men also hold some assumptions about female sexual functioning that are a little out of date, if not frightening. One man told me that his wife had never had a vaginal climax. He said, "Can you imagine that? The problem has to be either her or me, and I've tried everything, so it must be her." The myth behind the concern was that a "real" climax had to be a vaginal one.

Despite the reported rarity of this experience by women,

both men and women continue to seek it and think they are failing as sexual beings if the vagina does not explode during intercourse. But the research continues to give evidence that the vaginal orgasm is more hype or myth. One report found almost 67 percent of the women in the study did not attain *any* kind of orgasm with consistency. Another 5 to 6 percent said they had never experienced an orgasm. The *Hite Report* recorded a higher percentage—11.6 percent—in that category.[11]

Both sexes should appreciate what they are experiencing rather than chase the elusive holy grail of orgasms.

Just as some husbands think their wives should have a vaginal orgasm, so some husbands expect their wives to have "standard" erogenous zones. When he touches the "right" spots and nothing happens, he wonders what's wrong with his wife. This myth undoubtedly has its roots in the locker rooms of junior and senior high schools. At least that's where I first heard it. It's what I call the blow-into-her-ear myth. I don't know whether there is any evidence that blowing into a woman's ear is a real turn-on or not, but it illustrates the problem. One woman's turn-on may be another woman's turnoff.

Although there are fairly standard sensitive areas for women, such as the genitals, breasts, mouth, and inner thighs, sexual arousal will not be the same for every woman. One man told me over coffee that he didn't know why caressing his wife's breasts didn't do anything for her, especially since she was very well developed! He was making a double assumption: (1) that all women's breasts should be equally sensitive, and (2) that the bigger the bust, the more intense the sexual encounter. (By the way, some men marry on the basis of such mythology, and then they can't figure out what happened.) These differences among women make them both fascinating and frustrating. Certainly partners need better communication about what is pleasing and not pleasing to both.

The last myth concerns what I call the aggressive tigress. If the first myth focused on the fact that many men marry an Earth Mother, this one centers on men's desire to be bedded in mistress fashion. My contention is that most men desire both a mother and a mistress in one package. I don't know of any man I have talked to or study I have read that doesn't come with the same male desire. Husbands wish their wives were more spontaneous, novel, experimental, and initiating. To desire this is one thing; to expect it as normative female behavior in bed is another. This myth is even more interesting because wives confess many of the same frustrations with their husbands. In a study done by Dr. Bernie Zilbergeld, he asserted, "Women said their men were quite resistant to trying new places, times, positions, and activities. For all their talk, men seem to be more inhibited than women and many women expressed a desire for less seriousness and more playfulness in sex."[12]

Men and women want the same thing from each other, but each sex is waiting for the other to initiate it. The myth for the man is that the woman will initiate variety and that she should be the aggressive tigress he wants. In reality, she probably won't be a tigress, but that doesn't mean she is opposed to assuming the role. In fact, she may be very much in favor of it. But if the man wants a tigress, he needs to communicate it and go for it.

I want to try to articulate where I see the husband in the bedroom in contrast to his wife of the nineties. Women are educated, literate, knowledgeable, and self-aware. Myths about the sexes have no place in today's world. Both sexes must cooperate and understand each other so that the bedrooms of America can be experienced more joyfully. Therefore, both sides must endeavor to drive out the old demonic lies that have been promoted about sexuality. Men and women must face realities about their personhood and their relationships. As one writer says,

> In sex . . . you may allow access to your emotions, to your interests and excitements. In doing so, you run the risk that this may be the start of real contact with the other person, a

kind of intimacy, with all the possibilities and dangers that intimacy implies.[13]

> *Sex functions as a mirror. We meet ourselves in it, and we often don't like what we see.*

Sex functions as a mirror. We meet ourselves in it, and we often don't like what we see. For her, sex is a romantic expression of the relationship, so the whole relationship—and the nature of the relationship at that moment—is on the line. For him, sex has become another area of performance-based identity, and many men are getting tired of it. He often longs for the same touching and caring that she desires but without having the fate of the whole relationship depending on every sexual experience.

Sex, for her, can be any experience of closeness, tenderness, and touching, whether it leads to anything more or not. Sex, for him, can also be those times of being held and holding, fondling his wife without thinking of his own pleasure, but there may still be the lingering, libidinal longing for passionate arousal by a passionate woman. It's always there somewhere, hovering over the experience and making the relationship more uneasy.

Sex, for her, is doing whatever she enjoys and delights in and knowing that her man is also delighted in her. Sex, for him, is enjoying her body but also connecting with her as a person. But he often doesn't know how to do that or to communicate his sexual fears and frustrations. It takes mature self-knowledge and a trusting relationship to do that. Many men have not developed this skill or do not feel secure enough about their sexuality or their relationship to reveal it.

Sex, for her, is being passive and letting her man make love to her. She doesn't like to be aggressive, and she wishes he would take more responsibility for being spontaneous and creative. Sex, for him, is just another area of life where nothing happens if he doesn't perform correctly. He wants to initiate and be more inventive, but he has to weigh the emotional rejection of his personhood if his sexual ideas are not shared enthusiastically. It's often easier and less painful emotionally to go back to the same old routine or do nothing at all.

What can make the bedroom less uneasy for men? Our manhood is on the line, even though it shouldn't be. What can we do as men to rid our bedrooms of these demons that so rob us of the joy possible through our God-given sexual abilities?

One of the foremost ancient sexual experts has given us a cryptic handbook for the joyful uniting of the sexes. His name is King Solomon, and his book is the Song of Solomon as found in the Bible. In his very descriptive and sexually explicit love story, five principles for lovemaking are evident.

Sexual Intimacy Takes Time

Early in Solomon's experience with the Shulamite, his bride-to-be, his descriptions of her are ever expanding. His first reference is short and simple; he sees only her eyes. The next reference is on the wedding night, and his descriptions run from her eyes to her teeth, lips, neck, and breasts. The final description, which takes place after the couple have been married for some time and even encountered some conflict, is by far the most intimate. Solomon discusses his wife's features from the bottom of her feet to the top of her head.

In counseling, I have talked with couples who expect the "bells and whistles" on their wedding night or shortly afterward. When that doesn't happen, they think something is wrong. Or one partner is more willing to explore sexual variety than the other, thus causing difficulty. My word from Solomon on sex is that the advanced stuff takes time to develop. Every couple has its own timetable. National averages and statistics need to be thrown to the wind. Go slow.

Sexual Intimacy Takes Timing

When it comes to sex, men can be very insensitive to their wives' schedules and different needs. Apparently King Solomon had the same difficulty. Solomon knocks on the door of his bride's chamber early one morning. Apparently, he had become sexually aroused on his way home from work, but as he makes his advance, she gives the traditional excuse. The headache actually has biblical precedent! Since she is not interested, Solomon, in typical male fashion, leaves. But as she thinks more about her man, she gets aroused.

This passage describes what happens in households all over the world every evening. It's a problem of timing. Solomon apparently forgot to look at the sundial in the courtyard. To enjoy sexual intimacy, couples must think through their schedules and find the best time to enjoy each other. I once taught with a man who told me he couldn't teach a class before 9:00 A.M. When I asked him why, he replied, "Because the kids are out of the house and on their way to school by 8:00 A.M." That's timing!

Sexual Intimacy Takes Talking

Our English word *intercourse* has to be prefaced by an adjective so that we can understand its proper meaning. In sexual intimacy, verbal intercourse is a basic prerequisite to sexual intercourse. In the Song, the partners communicate what is pleasing about the other. They praise each other's physical attractiveness, verbalize their desires, and communicate as their lovemaking proceeds. The verbal communication creates the romantic atmosphere in which sexual intimacy can blossom.

Sexual Intimacy Takes Trust

This ultimate self-giving requires a relationship of trust, a relationship in which playful expression and comfortable exploration can take place. The Shulamite requests this relationship from Solomon and even perhaps has an alarming dream concerning its absence. Throughout this love poem is the consistent theme of not allowing sexual love to be aroused until it can be totally satisfied. The context in which it can be achieved is that of a secure love relationship in marriage. Many problems experienced by couples stem from lack of trust. Sometimes, one partner has broken trust through sexual affairs; sometimes, the inability to climax has its source in not being able to completely give oneself to a person in whom there is not complete trust.

Sexual Intimacy Takes Time Away

Our technological society has created an abundance of time-saving devices, but they only push us faster in the laser lanes of life. If we desire to have a satisfactory sex life, we are going to have to learn to slow down a bit. When the Shulamite is caught up in her love for Solomon, she initiates some time away with him. She says, "Let's go into the country, find a cute place to stay, see if the leaves have turned, and make love!" I believe Solomon was packing, canceling appointments, and getting someone to stand in for him at important meetings. Time away from kids, responsibilities, and friends is essential to a growing, intimate sexual relationship. The couple need time to explore, time to develop new trust, time to talk, and time to develop the rest of these principles.[14]

Although keeping these principles will not guarantee bells and whistles on the marital bed, they provide some parameters from which the sexual relationship may become more fulfilling and less uneasy for men. However, they will not remove the inherent tensions placed on men in our culture. Manhood is uneasy, and it has not been the goal of this book to say the tensions or difficulties are magically removed by merely adhering to correct or even biblical principles. The reality of manhood is still there, and that encompasses the bedroom. Andrew Greeley has expressed well men's sexual bind:

In a culture like ours, the position of the male is at best precarious. He is expected to be two different persons. In the world of career, he is supposed to be vigorous, hard-driving, ruthless, ambitious, committed to success. On the other hand, when he goes into the family psychological environment he is expected to be gentle, compassionate, tender, sympathetic. In other words, in the world of profession, career and job, a man is forced to be aggressive even though he has little confidence in his abilities in this direction; and in his relationship with his wife and family, he is expected to be communal even though he has little confidence in these skills either. To make matters worse, occupational success is taken in our society to be a proof of masculinity. You prove your ability in one way in the world in which you work and in quite a different way in the marriage bed and at the dinner table. The usual unsatisfactory compromise is something that is not aggressive enough for the world of career and not expressive enough for love making. The man approaches his wife like she is a client to whom something must be sold, realizing probably that this is not the way to do it, but not knowing for sure what he should be doing. . . . The net result is a male who in the genital encounter is neither aggressive enough or caring and communal enough.[15]

That's why the bedroom is so uneasy! But if the bedroom is uneasy, what happens in the bedroom creates another arena where competency and male identity are constantly evaluated. Becoming a father is the easy part, but *being* a father is not easy.

many men share my friend's dilemma. Children may have multiple father figures, no father at all, or a father in a distant land. On the other end of the relationship stands the father. Whether he is a single father who tries to parent from a distance or tries to be father and mother to his kids at home, a stepfather who cares for children with whom he has no genetic link living in his home, or a father who is still married to his first wife and has children of his own making, parenting is not easy. I'm not sure that parenting has ever been easy, but fathering has taken on new pressures and responsibilities and has become an altogether new reality. The expectations, frustrations, financial commitments, the binds between work and parenting responsibilities, and the lack of healthy contemporary models all come together to make for uneasy fathering.

Change is never easy. But when it comes to the art and skills of fathering, much has changed since my father's generation. My "birthing" experiences illustrate the quantum-leap changes that have occurred during my life span. When our first child was born, I was relegated to the waiting room. I had no option. The hospital administrators had deemed it inappropriate for fathers to observe the experience of childbirth.

Could we as men not handle it? Were we in the way? Or might we do something stupid? I don't know, but there I was in the smoky waiting room with my mother-in-law, anxiously looking up at every gowned person who came through the door. To be perfectly honest, I didn't feel slighted or treated like a second-class citizen. It never entered my mind that I *should* be with my wife. I had been raised with all the television imagery of the nervous father pacing the waiting room until the doctor or nurse enters and says, "It's a boy! Congratulations!" I didn't have any feelings of animosity toward the hospital staff or feelings of regret because I wasn't there when my firstborn daughter, Charis, arrived. It was just the spirit of the times. A father's place was in the waiting room.

Within two years, much had changed. It was the middle seventies, and attitudes favored more fatherly participation.

When Ashley, my second daughter, arrived, I was allowed into the delivery room, camera in hand—immediately *after* she was born. (I forgot to put film in the camera so we missed the event for recorded memory's sake.) I was allowed to hold my newborn daughter, kiss my wife, and share the moment to a greater extent than with my first child. I was even allowed to be with Cinny until the time she was wheeled into the delivery room. Labor rooms were no longer off-limits to fathers. It was a different experience to be there with my wife, listening to the moans and groans of women on the other side of the curtain. I enjoyed being with my wife, and even though the camera failed to record the event, the pictorial impressions are recorded in my mind.

Four years later, we finally arrived as a couple. It was almost the eighties. The ten-year period between our first child and our last one marked a critical change in the hospital's view of dads and in the amount of involvement dads could have and want to have in the birthing process. I remember when Cinny announced she was pregnant with number three, we were approached by a nurse in our church who said, "Of course, you want to do the right thing for your baby by having a home birth!" A home birth! I remember thinking, *That's a long way from the waiting room. Am I really ready for this?*

From the waiting room at the hospital to a sort of do-it-yourself home birth is quite a transition. The attitudes had so changed in ten years that I realized very quickly there was certainly something wrong with me and I was not the kind of man who really loved his wife or kid-to-be if we wanted the traditional dad-in-the-waiting-room birth. Since my perceived masculinity and my wife's maternal credibility were at risk, we decided to go along with the home birth classes, just to see if we could pass the course. I think we failed!

We took our pillows to class one night a week for several weeks and with a few other couples practiced our breathing and coaching techniques. The content of the sessions was an interesting mix of medical advice and naturalistic philosophy.

The natural home environment with low lights, the other kids watching the big event, the husband standing with his wife, caressing and kissing her and finally catching the new arrival—all were part of the package deal. We hung in there until one couple brought a home movie of a previous birth. I must say I was somewhat overwhelmed by sitting next to the very woman I was watching on the screen. As I looked around, everybody seemed to think it was really special. On the way home that night, Cinny and I vowed to each other that there would be no movies of number three!

We finally compromised and decided to go natural but do it at the hospital. We had been taught that the best thing for the child was a drug-free birth, and we were committed to that. But more important, I could be with Cinny in the actual delivery and coach her through labor. I was looking forward to it. Then the long-expected due date came and went. Nine months became ten months.

The prenatal care doctor began to get concerned. He told us it was unsafe to allow the pregnancy to go any further and suggested inducing labor. Induced labor meant drugs! Our birth class nurse was furious. How could we do that to our child? Didn't we love our unborn more than that? How could we be such failures?

However, we followed the physician's advice, admitted Cinny to the hospital, and were placed into a birthing room. The birthing room surprised me. It didn't have that sterile-hospital room look or feel. Colorful designs were on the walls, and stereo music was piped in. I was given a mask, a gown, and shoe coverings; all the stuff the doctors and nurses wear. I was a coach!

I left Cinny briefly to get something to eat, but I was soon paged: "Mr. Hicks, your wife is ready!" She was ready to give birth, ready for me, the coach! By the time I reached the birthing room, a nurse of thirty years' experience was with my wife. She said, "You'd better start your coaching. She's in a lot of pain." We went through the breathing exercises we had rehearsed many times before. But Cinny kept moaning, and she was in obvious pain. We hadn't anticipated the amount of pain a ten-pound baby could produce.

Finally, the wise nurse said to me, "I don't want to interfere with your convictions, but one shot could make a big difference here." I looked at Cinny and asked, "Do you want a shot for the pain?" "Yes!!!!" she moaned. The shot was heaven-sent. Graham was born. The doctor let me cut his cord, and I laid our newly born son on my wife's chest. It was a special moment.

None of my children is more significant than the others. They are all unique and special because they are *our* kids. But they illustrate how the attitudes toward birthing and fathering changed in just one decade.

Myths of Fathering

Have these changes made fathering more easy or more difficult? Change is never easy. Every social change brings with it new frustrations and expectations. It also means new myths develop and become a part of the social mythology. Many social myths surround fathering, but here are some that have made my fathering more uneasy. As I talk with other men, listening to their concerns and frustrations, I find these are shared. Some myths make men angry. They are enraged by the pressure these often unrecognized and unarticulated myths produce in their lives.

The Family First

When the men came back from World War II, many felt they had missed out on receiving an education and getting a jump on their careers. It was as if a whole generation of men (in agreement with their wives) made a mental contract, saying to themselves and others, "I will devote myself fully to my job and career, and you, as wife, will take care of the kids. I am the provider, and you are the nurturer."

The contract worked, for the most part, until the sixties. Then women demanded equal access to careers; they were tired of bearing all the nurturing responsibilities without helping hands from the men. The emerging adult children of the sixties were saying, "Thanks, Dad, for the money, but who are you? I don't know you. I never see you." One child of this generation told me, "I was the kid my dad missed because my formative years hit his career peak, and he was just never there." The pendulum began to swing back the other direction, as it should have. Researchers revealed, "Kids need nurturing fathers"; mothers proclaimed, "We need help at home"; and fathers said, "We don't want work to dominate our lives." The church woke up and asserted, "The family comes first."

My initial introduction to Christianity was largely through this "family first" message. I appreciated the family emphasis as a needed corrective to the earlier strict role for men. I wanted to put my family first. I went to seminars and conferences that helped me organize my time and arrange my life around whatever priorities I had for my life. My highest priority—next to God—was always my family. I taught it, encouraged it, and believed in it. But over time, as I seriously examined how I lived and the other expectations placed upon me as a man and a person, I started to sense the inherent mythology of the commitment. In one sense, it was as strict a role model as the one of the previous generation. However, the workability of the commitment had serious problems. Two illustrations may clarify my point here.

Establishing a hierarchy of priorities that are genuine expressions of your values and commitments is necessary and helpful for your own clarification. However, knowing your priorities will not help you make every decision confronting you. I remember walking out the door of our house to have an evening date with Cinny. Because my wife was (and is) a priority to me, and because time with her was also a priority, I would schedule dates with her. No matter what I was asked to do, I would protect the time allotted to her. We were on our way to dinner when the phone rang. A very young member of my church had been hit by a car, and the parents could not be reached. I was his pastor, and a friend had phoned to see if I knew where the child's parents might be. On my priority commitment list, my wife was higher than my work at the church. But I felt an emotional bind; I knew where I should be. Cinny read my mind and, without a further thought, said, "Let's go to the hospital." Dinner was delayed; our date changed. The ministry of the church overrode my "family first" commitment.

A second example illustrates the flip side. I had been out of town for several weeks due to military training. When I returned, I had several back-to-back evening meetings at the church. The third one in a row was an important elders' meeting. Some crucial issues were facing the church, I was on the staff of the church, and the issues to be discussed affected my area of responsibility. I needed to be there to give my point of view, defend my position, and vote.

However, Cinny called my office that afternoon and informed me the principal had called. There was a problem at school with our son. Then she added, "I think your son needs you. You've been gone a lot." I had been well trained. I still remember my mentor, Dr. Howard Hendricks, saying, "When my wife tells me I'm too busy, I take it as from God." God was speaking to me then. But I felt uneasy. I thought, *Do I miss this crucial-to-the-life-of-the-church meeting to be home with my son?* I finally picked up the phone, called the chairman of our church board, told him what had happened and how I felt about the issues on the table for the meeting that night, and informed him I wasn't going to be there. I properly went home.

The "family first" myth, as good a corrective as it was for a time, has its downsides as well. We live in the present, and that means the needs of the moment change. As a man, I have many responsibilities, dreams, ambitions, commitments, values, beliefs, likes and dislikes. All are part of who I am as a person, even a Christian person. Work is important to me; doing well at it is important to me. Having friends is important to me. Getting enough rest and relaxation is important to me. Enjoying my reading, writing, and ministry is important to me. My family and marriage are important to me. Trying to arrange all these things in some absolute hierarchical fashion is not only impossible to practice consistently but also very unhealthy and insensitive to many other responsibilities and to myself.

I hope we have the kind of people in our lives who can recognize that we can't be at every important meeting due to family problems or a spouse who realizes that there are times when she cannot be first because of other urgent needs or responsibilities. Placing the family first is a great ideal, but it makes for unrealistic living and parenting. I don't love my kids any less when I am at work, and I don't believe I am being irresponsible because I am not present at every work-related meeting that needs me.

> *Placing the family first is a great ideal, but it makes for unrealistic living and parenting.*

Keeping the family first is a nice corrective for a generation of fathers that missed out on family life, but in my experience and the experience of many others, consistently practicing the doctrine is difficult. Maybe it's time to admit how we really live and demythologize the belief. Only God can be first in my life, and I trust Him to give me the wisdom to know what I need to do in every situation. This means looking realistically at all my responsibilities and concerns and trying to do the best I can in light of all my priorities. I am an Air National Guard reservist, and we have a saying that goes, "Between our civilian jobs, our family, and the Guard, at least one of them is mad at us every day. Some days it's two out of three. Other days it's all three!" That's reality, the reality that makes fathering at times uneasy.

The Father's Responsibility for the Spiritual Growth of the Whole Family

A second myth that I cut my spiritual teeth on was this: by virtue of being born male, I get to be the "head" of the family. Early on in my marriage that was flattering and ego glorifying. I thought, *Wow, I'm in charge!* The older I get, though, the more I recognize this belief for what it really is—a myth.

The problem with writing about my feelings on this subject is that I place myself in the position of being viewed as irresponsible to this family role. In some circles, questioning this assumption of family life puts you at odds with many. But I know many men who are tired of the pressure of having the sole responsibility for the behavior, attitudes, and life-styles of each family member. When their children reach their teens and have problems, when a son divorces or gets arrested, or when a daughter becomes pregnant out of wedlock or gets addicted to drugs, some men are blamed for not being the spiritual leader and nurturer of the family, and they feel like failures at their task.

John White, a noted Christian author and psychiatrist, observes,

> Until the twentieth century parents knew how to bring up their children. . . . If their children turned out badly, they were more inclined than we to blame the children and not themselves. . . . The net result of the deluge of child-rearing articles both religious and secular has been to create two generations of parents who have been anxious, guilty and uncertain of themselves.[1]

He goes on to show that in this family-enlightened age, we as parents are looking for a direct cause-effect relationship in parenting and fathering. He states,

We have been looking at this law of cause and effect. I have been arguing as though if we knew enough, which we don't, we could come up with some sort of formula. We could say John is the way he is because 33.7% of the factors have to do with parenting, 22.4% with general cultural influences, 21.0% with genetic mechanisms of various types and 22.9% with other factors. But what about John? Did he have no real say? Did he merely feel as though he were making choices? Is John nothing more than the sum of the influences that were brought to bear on him? Or is he something more? Is he a person who made real choices? As a Christian I believe we can never "explain" John scientifically. John is John. He has a will. He chooses. He is pursuing a path he himself selected. . . . We have seen that careful thinking tells us that we can neither take all the credit for our children when they turn out well nor all the blame when they turn out badly.[2]

I don't know why the child's outcome is linked to parenting effectiveness. But in my experience the responsibility for the kid's failure is laid directly at the father's feet. Although the mother probably feels the failure more intensely, at least in the church the father is considered the one who does not have his family under control. After all, he is the spiritual leader of the family. And the basic understanding is that success as a spiritual leader means a direct cause-effect relationship between sterling character in the father and sterling character in the children. If there is a problem with the kid, there must be a problem with the parent or the parenting process.

> *Although the mother probably feels the failure more intensely, at least in the church the father is considered the one who does not have his family under control.*

Don't be misled into thinking I downplay the significance of the father's role in the parenting process. His contribution to the child's life is profound. Michael Lamb, a University of Utah professor and a leading researcher on the father's role in child development, remarks,

As far as sex role development is concerned, the father's masculinity and his status in the family are correlated with the masculinity of his sons and the femininity of his daughters. However, this association depends on the fathers having sufficient interaction with their children—thus the extent of the father's commitment to childrearing is crucial. One of the best established findings is that the masculinity of sons and femininity of daughters is greatest when fathers are nurturant and participate extensively in childrearing.[3]

But having underscored the father's distinctive contribution to the child's life, he then points out,

It is obvious that fathers are but one element in the complex and multifaceted process of socialization. Both parents contribute to the psychological development of their offspring, and it is unlikely that their contributions are independent. Dyadic models (two people alone), although simpler to conceptualize, seriously distort the psychological and sociological realities of the environments in which children develop. Since children have to be integrated into an extremely complex social system, the process of socialization itself must be complex, flexible, and multifaceted. It should not be surprising that such a process demands the complementary participation of several persons.[4]

Is the father solely responsible for everything that happens in the home? If he is, it is no wonder so many fathers are expressing their indignation about this unrealistic expectation. The father is responsible to be a father to his children, to be a nurturing influence in their lives, but not to the exclusion of the mother or other significant adults. Even the Scriptures seem to highlight joint responsibility of spiritual and moral leadership in the home. Both fathers and mothers are to be involved in teaching, correcting, and influencing (Prov. 1:8; 4:3; 6:20; 10:1; 17:25; 31:1, 26–27; 1 Thess. 2:7, 11). It's too big a job for one individual. Even single parents must realize that they need other significant adults in the child's life to be a part of character formation. Ultimately, the child must decide what course of life to pursue.

Much contemporary Christian teaching on fathering assumes that the parent controls the child's choices. The assumption is that the goal of fathering and parenting is control of the child. The Scriptures emphasize the issue of control, but as I see it, control is not the goal of fathering. If control is the goal, choice must be taken away, and without the freedom of choice, the child can never adequately develop. Howard Hendricks has said on numerous occasions, "Anytime I do something for my child that he is capable of doing himself, I am making him an emotional cripple." I would add, anytime I make decisions for my child that he is capable of making for himself, I am thwarting the maturing process. But this statement sends chills up the doctrinal spines of many fundamentalist Christians. If a dad does not have his kids under control, how can he be a man of God?

The Scriptures warn about what a father can potentially do to his children. The apostle Paul, the church's first domestic theologian, revealed that fathers had the potential to literally crush the spirit of children, to embitter and exasperate them. He also cautioned that in their sincere attempts to nurture spiritual values, fathers could provoke their children to anger (Col. 3:21).

I have known many of these children as adults. They are from strict religious backgrounds; they are preachers' and missionaries' kids; and most of their choices about church, spiritual values, and morals were taken away from them. For the interest of their father's career or image, they had to be good little Christian kids—whether they wanted to or not. It's not surprising when they finally had the opportunity to leave the home, they abandoned the religiosity of their parents.

Spiritual leadership does not imply controlling the child's choices. Even in the qualification list for leaders in the church, the text says, "Keeping his children under control with all dignity" (1 Tim. 3:4, NASB). (The word used for dignity conveys the idea of holding the head up high.) Control is not the goal; the father should strive to have a relationship of respect and dignity with the child.

I have lost my dignity too many times with my own kids. They don't do what I want them to do, so I finally yell and scold them. I demean their value by universalizing their childish behavior: "You never . . . you always. . . ." And I watch their little faces tilt downward as they look at the floor. I have succeeded. I have them under my control! But what has happened? We no longer have a relationship of dignity. All my respect for them—and their respect for me—is gone. I have not succeeded; I have failed. But many in the Christian community applaud my victory in getting them "under control."

> **The view of the father as the all-powerful spiritual leader of the family, controlling the behavior of the family members, is a myth.**

The view of the father as the all-powerful spiritual leader of the family, controlling the behavior of the family members, is a myth. I don't think men want the sole responsibility for what happens to their kids. No more than the mothers want it. I know hundreds of men who love their kids and are doing the best they can to be some kind of leader in the home, but rarely do they have their kids or anything else under control. I also believe there is little relation to how well a dad relates to his kids and how well they will do in life. We are not dealing with computer functions when we come to parenting.

Punch the right function key on a computer, and the proper result appears on the screen. Parenting isn't at all like that because parents are coping with individuals, not automatons.

In the ancient book on parenting wisdom, King Solomon acknowledges his limitations with his own son. He admonishes,

> My son, *if* you receive my words,
> And treasure my commands within you,
> So that you incline your ear to wisdom,
> And apply your heart to understanding;
> Yes, *if* you cry out for discernment,
> And lift up your voice for understanding,
> *If* you seek her as silver,
> And search for her as for hidden treasures;
> *Then* you will understand the fear of the LORD,
> And find the knowledge of God
> (Prov. 2:1–5, emphasis added).

Solomon realizes that all he can do is to encourage his son to take a certain path. The outcome is conditional because it is the son's choice. I don't have the ability to cause my children to love God and be discerning and understanding about life. I can only model that kind of life and encourage it for them. Ultimately, the choice is theirs. Solomon admits that fathering is conditional, not a cause-effect relationship.

Another myth is becoming more predominant. It's what I call the superfather myth.

The Superdad

Supermoms are fairly well known. They can juggle careers and marriage and still be regulars at the garden club, attend benefit dinners, make their own Christmas gifts, preside over the PTA, and sponsor the cheerleaders. It was just a matter of time until the dads also got into the act. When the new really-involved-with-his-kids kind of father emerged, a logical expectation was that soon dads would become superdads. Oh, there have always been stage dads who lived for their sons' sports achievements or their daughters' swim team medals. I've also known men who found more enjoyment and meaning in life by coaching the Little League than in working at their careers. They have always been present in communities. But now I see another kind of male who makes my fathering even further uneasy. He's the superdad.

Superdad is the church's, Little League's, and school's ideal man. He is involved, present, and available; he is the perfect volunteer. He teaches a children's Sunday school class, coaches the soccer team, raises money for the Girl Scouts, attends all parent-teacher conferences, and still has time to be successful in his career and his marriage.

Men like me never know how he does it. I'm probably a bit jealous of this guy's involvement and energy, but at the same time the whole image seems more out of *Father Knows Best* than the normal busy life I lead. I'm a one-trick pony; it's hard for me to do more than one thing well. Therefore, when I see the need for another coach on my son's soccer team, I always feel a pinge of guilt—especially when my wife says, "Honey, you can do it." It's almost beside the point that I know very little about soccer. The guilt surfaces the myth that dads who love their sons will coach soccer, whether they know anything about it or not. I cannot merely go to my son's soccer game and enjoy his involvement; my presence is not enough. I need to be involved with him; I need to be a coach.

The guilt also strikes at one of my most favorite fatherly experiences—the parent-teacher conference. Some teachers make me feel more like a child than a man. The teacher makes me sit on one of those little chairs while she goes over all the areas where my child is not working up to ability. Finally, the teacher looks up from the less-than-acceptable work and says, "Now, what are *you* going to do about this?"

None of my kids has done well in math, so I particularly hate getting into that area of performance. The implication is always the same: "Now, Mr. Hicks, you need to spend more time with —— and help with the math homework. Are you going to help correct these deficiencies?" I wonder what would happen if I really spoke my mind and said, "No. I can't balance my checkbook, and I haven't used geometry, algebra, or trig since the day I finished each course. I don't do anything mathematical now without a calculator, an attorney, and a CPA."

The problem is that there is not a mathematical mind in our household. Somehow, we missed this gift when it was being distributed. It doesn't really matter how much time I spend with my kids "helping" them do their math homework. Frankly, they surpassed my understanding of math in the third grade, but try to admit that to a junior-high or senior-high teacher. Express it and you'll find how fully the superdad myth has been accepted. Besides there is an unacknowledged contract between parent and teacher. Most teachers know how busy parents are, but they also know the power they have in The Grades. The parent equally realizes that most of what the kid is learning (big assumption) will be lost, irrelevant, or outdated the moment he finishes the class, but The Grades mean college. So an unconscious contract is forged. Parents push the grades for the sake of college while not blowing the whistle on the reality that the information is not life changing. It creates quite a bind for fathers who want to tell the truth to their kids.

When Charis was a senior in high school, she asked, "Dad, how often do you use algebra?" I faced a dilemma. Should I be honest and tell her the truth: "I never use it"? If I told her that, I feared she would no longer be motivated to do her homework and take the class seriously. If she didn't take the class seriously, she'd get a bad grade, which might affect her acceptance into the "right" college. On the other hand, if I lied, I'd really be in a mess. I knew her next question would be, "How and where do you use algebra?" In trying to fix one problem I would create a bigger one. I'm not sure what super-dads do, but my perception is that every night they sit around the dining room table with their kids, involved with their homework, even when football is on TV!

This whole chapter could be my rationalization for often feeling like a fatherly failure, but I don't think so. I believe enough research suggests that anyone who is obsessively concerned with the behavior or activities of others (even one's kids) is not a healthy individual. Unfortunately, schools, churches, and organizations seem to reward this obsessive involvement and deem the obsessed individual a model parent. David Elkind has written extensively about "the hurried child":

> Today, disturbed children have to be seen, evaluated, and helped within the context of an overwhelmingly stressful environment. If anything, the children we see in the clinic today are more like the shell shock victims of battle than the neurotic children of the past. In a sense, war is to adults what hurrying is to children—an enormous stress which brings much harm and some good.[5]

He explains how parents "hurry" their kids into sports to make up for inadequacies in their own lives:

> Children thus became symbols or carriers of their parents' frustrated competiveness. . . . The parent can take pride in the child's success or blame him. . . . In any case, the parent soon vicariously invests more of a commitment in the child than his or her own life.[6]

Superdads may be well motivated for children's success, and our culture may consider them involved, concerned parents. But the things they are concerned about are predictable. The pressure and resultant stress always come from adult values, usually what we parents hold as respectable, successful, and useful. Compared to socially desirable activities, such as athletic competition, clubs, and organized events centered on school and church, walking in the park, sitting on a riverbank fishing, and building a fort in the backyard can never measure up. Those activities are hard to justify in a performance-driven society; they certainly won't get anyone into college. But nonproductive, nonprogrammed play is important for children's growth and creativity.

If I am jealous of superdads, it's only for a moment. When I take a longer view, I see my own dad, who often said, "Come with me." And we went! I had nonperformance time with my dad. It didn't really matter what we did or where we went; I was with him. He wasn't a superdad, and neither am I.

The Bankrolling Father

I live on Philadelphia's Main Line. Before I moved to this elite suburb, I thought "main line" was something people did with drugs. However, now the Main Line brings to mind an entire image and philosophy of life. Oh, the people in this suburb joke about it and for the most part don't think or admit they are part of the social and economic conformity. But they are. So am I. Whether I like it or not, I am bound to an economic expectation about life that affects my children as well as me.

I shouldn't live where I live. Fundamentally, I can't afford it. Yet, I was originally called to a church in this area, so here I am. I live on the Main Line, my kids go to Main Line schools, their friends are Main Line kids, and their friends' fathers are Main Line attorneys, doctors, CEO's, CPA's, and noted politicians and authors.

I like where I live. It's a beautiful, historic area established by "old money." Rolling estates have been subdivided to allow newer moneyed families to move into the area and allow me the privilege of living here, also. In one regard I feel comfortable here. I'm an upper-middle-class person with a college education, a professional who is somewhat well-read and intelligent. I can compete until it comes to money.

One of my pet peeves about most of what is written about the family today is that the literature often ignores the economic pressures and their complications affecting the family. I can go into almost any bookstore and pick up a book about some couple who got back together after having their marriage on the rocks or read a book about how to get my priorities straightened out and solve my management problems at home. But they rarely address me where I live. Many of the suggestions require money—and an abundance of it. What's the going rate for marriage counseling? In my area it's around seventy-five dollars per hour for a professional. It takes money to get your marriage together. How about marriage enrichment retreats? At least two hundred dollars for a weekend! I wonder what the poor do?

When we moved into our house on the Main Line, we got the cheapest one around. But cheap comes at a price eventually. It needed a lot of work. Occasionally, friends would come by to see what needed to be done. Some responded by saying, "Oh, that's easy to fix. I know the best carpenter on the Main Line. I'll give you his phone number. I'm sure he could work you in." It was easy to fix—if you wanted to pay the Main Line rates. Others were more realistic. One dear friend showed up and wallpapered one whole room during a weekend.

All of this is my way of bringing up another myth: being a good father means being able to provide for one's kids everything they want or everything the other kids in the neighborhood are getting. That myth makes my fathering uneasy.

The older my kids get, the more I struggle with this issue. The reason is obvious: the price tags keep getting significantly larger than my ability to pay. It began with diapers, then little shoes, then bicycles, then teenage auto insurance rates, and finally college. I remember sitting down with one college financial officer who was very polite and very encouraging. He assured me, "Now, Mr. Hicks, what we do here is to put together a financial package of grants, scholarships, loans, and funds the parent can provide. How much of this $16,000 bill can you provide?" I stuttered, "How about $1,000?" The young, neatly trimmed, and well-dressed financial officer smiled and replied, "Well, we'll need a little more than that." What a fatherly failure I am! It wasn't too long ago that I worked for less that $16,000 a year with more discretionary money left over than I now have.

This feeling of failure strikes very deep within a man. As I watch my fellow masculine professionals take their families to Aspen for Christmas, buy brand-new cars for their graduating seniors, and fly them here and there at will, it is easy to conclude that good fathers do those things for their children. Jesus alludes to the fact that good fathers give good gifts to their children (Matt. 7:9–11). But I have never been in the financial position to be able to give such gifts to my children. We have lived with the reality of having "boring" Christmases at home, owning twenty-year-old VW bugs, and driving ridiculous distances to get places because it was cheaper than flying.

Although I know within my soul that a bankrolling father is not necessarily a good father, I have been so nurtured on the American cultural myth of the male as provider and protector that I still feel like a failure when I can't give my kids what they want or what I wish I could give them. In our society today I think many men are facing an ever-growing and permanent downward mobility. It's hardest for those of us who have been raised with middle- and upper-middle-class expectations.

In a study of downwardly mobile families, Katherine Newman writes, "Downward mobility strikes at the heart of the 'masculine ideal' for the middle class. When the man of the house has failed at the task that most clearly defines his role, he suffers a loss of identity as a man."[7] She adds the dimension of the working wife who has to make up the financial inadequacies created by the husband: "When this is coupled with the admirable efforts of a wife to salvage the situation by going to work, the man's response may be intensified by feelings of impotence and rage culminating in abuse."[8]

Newman also sees that the children raised in such environ-

> **In our society today I think many men are facing an ever-growing and permanent downward mobility.**

ments think of themselves as victims, even though it is not always clear who or what has victimized them.

The financial pressure enrages men and makes the kids feel like victims of unseen and often misunderstood forces. This has serious implications. As a Christian, I know that one cannot love both God and mammon, and the material reality is not the reality in which we are to put our trust. But we live in a material world, our kids live in a material world, and money solves *some* of life's problems. I am tired of feeling like a failure because I can't provide all I desire for my family.

I suggest that the bankrolling father glorified in our culture is a myth. Even the lives of many rich and famous Christians are shot through with lies about reality. Most of the people I know who are honest about their lives or how well they live will admit they are one month away from financial disaster. They are overleveraged, overdrawn, overloaned, and overburdened with debt; they are doing the best they can just to stay afloat.

I appreciate their honesty. It lets me know that if I choose to have less stuff or give less stuff to my kids, I have not failed my kids. I hope one day they will realize they had a father who tried his best to give them what he could, and in the final analysis they may recognize that the greatest gift was the gift of having a father in their lives, despite all his failures.

After extensively interviewing the famous and the infamous, Christopher Andersen, the senior editor of *People* magazine, wrote a book on what he says they all eventually got around to talking about . . . their fathers. His concluding remarks provide a realistic outlook:

Being a father is not a job, and anyone who says it is or thinks it is communicates that to his child. Fatherhood is a state of being, and not only is it not that difficult, but the joys and rewards invariably outweigh all difficulties. Home should not be a training camp. Approval or disapproval of our "success" at raising a child should not be sought from the outside world. A father lives with a woman, and he lives with his children. If there is ample opportunity for gentle symbiosis, for honest concern and warmth, then that is enough. Father does not teach his child to be creative, intelligent, humane. Creativity, intelligence, humanity, can only be allowed to develop. The contribution Father makes is one of subtle guidance. Contrary to what is being widely preached by the high priests of pop psych, it is futile to try to get Mom and Dad to agree on every aspect of rearing the kids. Every household will have its pushover and its taskmaster, its grudge holder and its peacemaker, its brooder and sprite. Parents are people too, and if they are forced to conform to some psychologist's idea of correct behavior, the child is quick to catch on.[9]

Uneasy Fathering in the Scriptures

I remember being in a seminary class one day when the professor threw out the question, "Who are some biblical personages you would consider a good father?" I quickly ran through my then limited biblical knowledge looking for such a parent. I was sure it was a legitimate question, and the problem was my lack of biblical education since I had gone to a university instead of a Bible college. However, I noticed many of my classmates, who had been raised in the church and had gone to Christian schools and Bible colleges, were also silent. Finally, the class clown blurted out, "Jesus." Everyone roared. Then after the laughter subsided, he said, "No, I was being serious. Jesus didn't have any kids, so He's the only perfect father!" His point picked up on the very issue the professor wanted to address: fatherly failure in the Scriptures.

One doesn't have to read far until he realizes that finding a good father is impossible. The Bible doesn't record sufficient detail about any father's kids to conclude that the kids turned out well because of the father's good parenting. What kind of father was the first father, Adam? One son killed his brother (Gen. 4:8). How about Noah? One of his sons did something unbecoming of a son to his father (Gen. 9:21–24). What about Abraham, the father of the nation of Israel? He couldn't wait to have an heir, so he fathered a child with a sexually available handmaiden (Gen. 16). Consider Isaac and Jacob. Isaac played favorites with his sons (Gen. 25:28), and Jacob was a deceiver whose sons committed murder, incest, and harlotry (Gen. 38:15) and sold their own brother into slavery (Gen. 30—50).

We can also think of Israel's kings as fathers. King Saul had mental and spiritual problems to such an extent that his own son became best friends with his archest enemy, David (1 Sam. 18). King David so neglected his son Absalom that Absalom had to lead a revolt against his father to get his attention (2 Sam. 15). David's son Solomon didn't do that much better with his kids. He loved the Lord, but he also loved his women, his armies, and his wealth. He had two sons who split the nation after his death. Israel never recovered from the split (2 Chron. 11). By the time we get to the New Testament, the writers are having to teach fathers what to do with their kids. The examples from the previous history weren't exactly sterling. They still aren't.

What's the conclusion? God is the only perfect Parent! He is the only good Father and even His kids (children of God) have throughout history gotten themselves into terrible messes. They have worshiped false gods, been immoral and ungodly, broken marriage covenants, murdered, stolen, and coveted. Most of God's experience with fathering has been uneasy. A look at the Scriptures indicates it wasn't easy for the biblical characters, either.

We can learn from God Himself what a good father looks

like. Because God is the creator of His human children, He is committed to them, no matter what they do. The prophets never accused Him of being a bad Father because His kids were so bad and ungodly. In fact, there exists a consistent emotional conflict within God Himself as to whether to get rid of the kids altogether (Hos. 1:6–9), but He always comes back and reaffirms His commitment to them to be their Father forever (Ezek. 16:60–63). He is a Father who hangs in there through thick and thin.

His fathering of us is not easy. But it encourages me to know that I'm not alone in thinking fathering is uneasy. In a small but significant way it makes my fathering easier. For this reason, I hang in there with my kids, no matter what they are going through.

Family researcher Urie Bronfenbrenner has stated on numerous occasions that the one most important aspect of fathering is the father's irrational commitment. Once when asked what he meant by "irrational commitment," he replied, "The father is crazy about his kids for no other reason than they are his kids."[10] Sometimes I feel teachers, school administrators, and parents are not sure of this phenomenon. Why do I feel guilty when I support my kids' position rather than that of the school, the Sunday school teacher, or even my spouse? In our psychologically aware society, an irrational commitment to your kids is termed "psychological denial" or "unwillingness to recognize their faults." I recognize them, but I'm still crazy about them because they are my kids.

Somehow, I think this is the way God views us as His kids. He knows our faults but has committed Himself to us in His Son. Was He living in denial or not facing reality by having His Son die for us so that we could genuinely be adopted into His family? I don't think so.

A Father's Contribution

Family therapist Carl Whitaker said, "Bad fathers make it easier for the kids to leave home and family." I agree that they make the physical leaving easier, but I'm not so sure about the emotional, mental, and identity issues related to separating. When I speak with men, they make it plain that their leaving has not been easy. Even their leaving and cleaving are complicated by the failures on the sending end in their homes of origin. As men spend more time being involved in the parenting process, they must certainly see what their role is and what their major contribution should be.[11] The father is critically important to the development of children. Michael Lamb's work, noted earlier, showed that the father plays a vital role in the moral development and sexual identity of both sexes.[12]

Emerging from this research is what many of us have felt for some time or have seen true in our own lives but didn't have much of a research base from which to prove it. Men make unique contributions to the parenting process. That doesn't mean the mother can't also contribute to it, but there are crucial developmental factors that only fathers bring to the parenting process. Just as the emotional development of the child during early childhood depends more upon the mother, so later in life, the father plays a more critical developmental role.

Seeing Life as a Whole

Children's lives are so structured by schools, churches, Little Leagues, and parents that playtime becomes another scheduled activity for them. We rush our kids from activity to activity—both theirs and ours. Travel time is hurried, and usually the radio is blaring to keep out the noise of life.

Something has been lost. How can I compare a ride to the store in our family car with my son to a father-son buckboard ride to town on Saturday one hundred years ago? Most men couldn't imagine having a long conversation with one of their kids. What did they talk about? Did they argue and disagree with each other? Did they ride in silence for long periods? Probably all of the above.

One thing I do know. The amount of time the child spent

with dad was more than it is today. Most men were not executives, engineers, or other kinds of technospecialists. They were specialists at life, and they imparted their philosophy of life.[13] David Elkind says that a life philosophy is one of the great "relief" values every kid needs:

> Everyone needs a philosophy of life, a way of seeing it whole and in perspective. The art of living is the most difficult task children have to learn, and they do this best if their parents have a way of looking at life as a whole. . . . Hurrying children into adulthood violates the sanctity of life by giving one period priority over another. . . . If we can overcome some of the stresses of our adult lives and decenter, we can begin to appreciate the value of childhood with its own special joys, sorrows, worries, and rewards.[14]

I hear Elkind saying that we as fathers need to take the time to savor our children's experiences and to provide a framework so that this can happen and develop. In these times the art of living is communicated.

Perhaps providing real spiritual leadership is developing the art of watching for and making the most of the teachable moment.

Perhaps providing real spiritual leadership is developing the art of watching for and making the most of the teachable moment. This means understanding some things about child and adolescent development and regarding most of what the child faces as predictable developmental crises: a two-year-old spills milk, a five-year-old says no to mother, a ten-year-old is clumsy at soccer, and a sixteen-year-old takes a drink or smokes. But we often make these moral and character issues. Fathers can provide a philosophy about life and growth that allows their kids the freedom to fail and develop under their protective hand.

I remember being asked to kick out a teenager from a youth conference because he was caught smoking pot. I had to call the father and tell him we were sending his son home because he was a bad influence on the other Christian kids. I was somewhat surprised by the father's reply: "OK, send him home. You know, boys will be boys." My first thought was, *What an out-to-lunch father. He ought to give that boy you know what.* Having been a father for almost twenty years now, I recognize he was a father who had an irrational commitment to his son and was crazy about him. He accepted his son even in his failure. By the way, today the son is a successful businessman.

Letting Go

A second contribution of fathers, especially to their daughters, is granting them freedom to grow up. In the book *Fathers and Daughters*, William Appleton notes that a primary characteristic of normal passage to adulthood is a daughter's time of conflict with her father.[15] This is an important but stressful time for both parties. However, the key developmental task from the viewpoint of the father is letting go of the child. The fatherly fears about allowing his little girl to make her own choices and suffer the consequences from them are not easy. They make our manhood difficult. Gordon Dalbey comments, "The major issue between father and daughter is one of separation: Can the father let go of the girl, express his confidence in her abilities and declare 'You are your own person.'"[16] We have seen this conflict portrayed in several modern films, *Coal Miner's Daughter, Norma Rae,* and *On Golden Pond.* All depict a daughter desperately trying to break free from her father in order to do what she wants to do, but still wanting the affirmation and acceptance as his daughter.

It is at this point that I have seen much of my own fatherly failure. I have had to face the reality of what I confessed to God upon the dedication of each of my girls to Him. My confession was that they are His and I am but a steward of His treasures. The confession implies that a time will come when my task will be finished (in terms of my active role). But a father values the daddy-love that is always special from his daughter. To see this change and to have her pull away make manhood and fatherhood uneasy.

In this separation, the father must let go. The process from the daughter's perspective is seeing her father in more biblical terms, terms that I as a former pastor have taught but never really wanted to face or admit. Jesus made it clear: "He who loves father or mother more than Me is not worthy of Me" (Matt. 10:37). If I want my children to be disciples of Jesus, they can no longer be my little girls, looking to me as a false idol. Gordon Dalbey illumines this daddy-love. In the separation he says, "The Daddy-god idol had fallen. Here lies death for idol-worshiping girls or the beginning of new life for faithful women and their fathers. For indeed, only when idols fall can God arise in lives."[17]

For a girl to have her own life and eventually bond with another man, she must separate from her father. Our role with our girls changes. We can no longer be the protector and provider and idol we once were. They have to grow up, and we must grow up and let go. We must give them over to our God and to other men. In their adult years, we must contribute an adult-to-adult relationship to their lives. We have to quit playing daddy with them (except when they want it) and to seek reconciliation with them if the separation process was overly painful and traumatic.

Calling Out

The relationships men form with their sons are different from those they form with their daughters. Competition between fathers and sons is often noted; emotional distance is fairly common. However, the unique contribution the father provides for his son is the critical male bonding and associated "calling out" of his manhood. Without this developmental task, the boy as a man may look for a "father" in mentors, friends, or even same-sex orientations.

Samuel Osherson's work, *Finding Our Fathers*, indicates that we as men often try to find the unaffirmed male within us through the rest of our life experiences with men and organizations. Most ancient cultures had cultural markers to clearly define and date manhood, but because our society lacks them, a boy must try to figure out on his own what this thing called manhood is all about. Thus, the father has the critical voice in the boy's life.

Male development is different from female development in the sense that girls do not have to leave mother to become women. They can remain friends for life, still do female things together (shopping, talking about clothes, decorating, and child raising), without giving up other important relationships. They have had their bonding time with mother, and this bonding does not have to be broken so that they can grow up and become women.

With a boy, the process is more complicated; a boy must separate from his mother and find his father. Cultural anthropologists have universally recognized this process; however, in the Western world all consciousness of it is usually ignored or laughed at. The closest custom related to it in our culture is the Jewish bar mitzvah. This ceremonial marker defines and makes a Jewish boy a man. In preparation for the event he must learn to read the Torah (Law) in Hebrew. Of course, he doesn't instantly become mature in terms of psychological or physical maturity. But through the ceremony, the Jewish community—primarily the men and his own father—calls forth his manhood.

Gordon Dalbey describes the practice of a Nigerian tribe. The men actually go to the hut of the boy and call him out from his mother to join the men of the community. The mother puts up a fight and cries over the loss of her son. The boy must choose between staying at home with his mother or joining the men. The men keep encouraging him to come out until he finally leaves. They then initiate him into the secrets of the tribe and "male secrets."[18]

The point of the tradition is clear. For the boy to become a man, he must give up mother and listen to the voices of men. It is interesting that the mother puts up a fight for the child, which is often the case. A mother must give up her precious little boy to the men; he must go with his father and the other men.

Today, I believe the only access to the male community (whatever it is) is through the father. But how can this process take place if a mother is a single parent? In this situation the noncustodial father must realize that even if he is at a distance, he is critical to the process. His son is listening for his voice. If the father is unwilling, a grandfather or uncles or male friends should be called upon to play this role.

Or what if you never went through this process? Knowing how to do something you haven't seen done is difficult. I don't think it is anything fancy or complex. It took place routinely in most cultures. Much of it happens by merely being there for your son and wanting an emotional bonding to occur with him. It's a funny thing about men. We think that showing open displays of affection toward our sons will make them sissies. The research shows just the opposite. Warm, friendly, nurturing fathers contribute strength and self-acceptance to their sons.[19]

> *It's a funny thing about men. We think that showing open displays of affection toward our sons will make them sissies. The research shows just the opposite.*

Our calling forth of our sons' manhood is gradual rather than ceremonial today. It happens in the hundreds of times we are together. With my son, it has been the times together talking about *Top Gun*, firing his BB gun, playing catch, and even having discussions after he has been disciplined. Each is a piece of the calling-out process.

A related problem concerns what to do when there is real animosity toward one's father for his failures in this regard. Dalbey offers keen insights:

> A man must beware the temptation to skirt the pain of being cut off from his father; to do so is to let that pain bind and control him from the deeper unconscious to which he banishes it. He must start where he genuinely is . . . he must beware of the companion temptation to judge and condemn his father for what the latter did not give him. The man who confesses his pain by bringing it to Jesus at the cross will begin to see that his father was not called out by his own father, so didn't know how to call out his son. One's father is not the oppressor, but a fellow victim, a brother in mutual need of manly affirmation.[20]

There are no perfect fathers. Our fathering will be marred. Fathering is not easy. It never has been; it never will be. We don't go to school to become fathers, and there is little on-the-job training for it. Most of us shoot from the hip, hoping we may do something right. It would be nice if the churches would help more in this area. But we as men have running conflicts with the church. It's not a place where we really feel comfortable, so even our Sundays are not easy.

CHAPTER 8

Uneasy Sundays

Or Why Men Feel So Out of Place in Church

———■———

A mother went into her son's room early one Sunday morning and tried to get him out of bed. After several attempts, she said, "Honey, you have to get up and go to church." He replied, "Give me one good reason why I have to go to church. The people at that church don't like me. Why should I go?" His mother declared, "Because you are the pastor!"

That's right. Even pastors feel out of place in church. I contend the reason is that the church—no matter what denomination—is essentially an institution that appeals more to women than to men. I am amused over all the current debate about ordaining women. It is as if women have never had any power in the church. But talk to any clergyman or look at most church records indicating percentages of men and women, and the truth comes out. Women exercise tremendous power in all churches by sheer numerical strength.

In the Catholic tradition, men pray to Mary; in the Protestant tradition, the word among ministers is to never take on the "women's group." In whatever tradition, the women are doing most of the intercessory work, and I don't mean prayer. I am told women read 80 percent of all Christian books. Even the ones written for men (like this one) will be read by women who buy them for their husbands.

Dr. Lyle Schaller, the nationally known church consultant, pointed to a changing trend that personally concerns him. He called it "the feminization of the church in almost all denominations." He noted that 60 to 62 percent of Sunday worshipers are female. In activities directly reflecting the life of the church, the gap between the sexes is even greater.[1]

How can this gap be explained? During one Sunday morning service, I looked around and asked myself, Does anything here really attract men? Is anything here distinctively masculine? I noticed robes, flowers, and things being repeated that most men couldn't relate to. Then I was given a quite skimpy meal. A Jewish friend told me after coming to my church for the first time, "The Lord doesn't set a very good table at your church, and I thought we Jews were chintzy. At least we really feed our people!" The picture has certainly changed from the Last Supper where Jesus enjoyed a good meal with His closest friends in the relaxed comfort of the Upper Room and in that context gave a new spiritual meaning to the meal. Today, this most important symbolic event has been reduced to pure formality with nothing earthy enough for most men to "feel."

By contrast, one of the most memorable Communion services I have ever experienced was held in the Australian outback. Because there was no pastor, the men of the church took turns leading the Communion service. A rugged miner was leading it the day I was there. He had all his notes on index cards, and in the middle of the ceremony all the cards fell to the floor. He tried to regain his composure, made an unsuccessful attempt to put the cards back in order, and finally started crying. He sobbed, "I wanted to do such a good job for the Lord." I looked around; there wasn't a dry eye in the place. I said to myself, Isn't this what Communion is all about, bringing our brokenness to the brokenness of Christ and finding the acceptance and forgiveness we so need in Him? After the service, we roasted an entire lamb on the spit and shared it.

The two images are far in distance and in concept. One service was flowery, formal, and predictable; the other was unpretentious and imperfect, with allowance for failure and human frailty. I would suggest one was feminine, the other masculine. What has brought about this large-scale feminization of the church, which makes men feel very much out of place? Some people might debate my observation about men on this point. Many men are "in church," but I am addressing whether or not they feel at home there.

During the process of my writing this book, my wife and I attended a couples' study with several other couples. The group represented many church traditions and levels of involvement. When they asked me to tell about the chapters of this book, I related an overview of each one. When I got to this chapter, I used the first title, "Why Men Hate Church." Of all the chapters I had shared, this one got the most reaction. Several men said piously, "I like church." But as the discussion proceeded, they finally got more honest. One admitted, "Yeah, I've never really felt comfortable there. I always feel like an outsider." As we went around the circle, all the men conveyed similar feelings, to the surprise of their wives. I suggest several possible reasons for these feelings.

The Minister as the Model of Spiritual Manhood

First, most men compare themselves to the image of the minister. The media's portrayal of the minister is one of the most often perpetuated exercises in systematic brainwashing. The clergyman is usually a priest or a priest type dressed in distinct garb, and of course, the producers choose an innocuous-looking, effeminate man for the part. He usually shows up in the perfunctory scenes of either marrying or burying, but even those scenes move quickly to get back to the "real" action. In movies the minister may exorcise demons as in *The Exorcist* (a job men really relate to) or be an ex-gunslinger as in a Clint Eastwood film. As I write, I cannot recall any recent depiction of what I would consider a normal cleric's life. To the average viewer, the minister lives in anonymity, on the fringe of life; he shows up only for cameo appearances at weddings, funerals, and presidential invocations.

To the average man, a clergyperson lives a life that he cannot comprehend, one with which he feels little in common. Most laymen probably wonder what he does all day long and if he really works hard. How could they know? I believe most businessmen in the church have lingering suspicions that their minister isn't earning his pay, and they think, *Wouldn't it be nice to have a job where you worked only one day a week?*

This perception is not true, but fantasies die hard. Most men identify very little with whatever the minister does all day. But the real problem lies in the fact that this life-on-the-fringe phantom (minister) becomes the model of both spirituality and masculinity for wives and women in general. The pastor is the perfect man, the spiritual man personified, the man a wife wishes her husband was like.

This is a terrifying aspect about the ministry—knowing that women in congregations are constantly comparing men like me to their husbands! If they only knew how often I wished I was in the husband's place, free of the foolish pettiness that sometimes characterizes the church and able to earn more money. Also, because most men in the church do not take the opportunity to get to know the pastor (they don't think there is anything to relate to), and because many pastors do not want to be found out (that they are just like other men), the men don't know anything about the real life of a minister. Therefore, the average churchman assumes that his wife's evaluation of his life by the standard of the pastor's life is correct. By that standard, he always comes up short. He is less spiritual and less committed, and he knows far less about the Bible.

The man in the pulpit becomes a subtle enemy to most men. There is nothing appealing about his life to other men. If honest, they may feel uncomfortable around a man who knows little about finances, the real world, and the temptations they face every day.

> *The man in the pulpit becomes a subtle enemy to most men.*

I remember being in the home of one of my early teachers in the Christian life. As a new convert, I had learned so much from him and genuinely appreciated his effect on my life. Since he was going to be out of town, he allowed a group of us to use his house for a dinner party. Having not been raised in the church, and not really knowing any minister in my twenty-one years, I didn't know what to expect in a minister's home. My picture was of a man who prayed and read the Scriptures all day. I guess I fully expected his house to reflect this picture.

Boy, was I disappointed. There wasn't one painting of Jesus. His kids had toys, even guns, and ski equipment was piled in the garage! I now thank God for this early imprinting on my soul. He was a man, not an effeminate phantom. I could relate to him. There was a point of masculine contact.

Dr. Donald Joy speaks of "the deformed male as the norm in our society," which has taken two forms. One is the macho man who deals with his deformity by compensating for his insecurity through "acting" manly rather than being manly. The other is the feminized deformed male who has given up on being a man and runs away from his manhood; he feels more comfortable on the feminine side of life.[2] Both greatly need to see normal manliness illustrated.

The minister holds a pivotal position in our culture to

— 159 —

model both realistic manhood and more realistic spirituality. For this to happen, however, a change of thinking on both sides of the pulpit or altar must occur. The average man asks, "What do I have in common with this man, and why should I listen to him?" The new males, the postwar babies who have been educated, if not brainwashed into thinking that integrity is related more to vulnerability than to performability, ask, "Are you for real? Do you struggle where I struggle? Are you going to shoot straight with me about your inner life?"

This seems easy to resolve, but remember I said that even pastors feel out of place in church. Sundays are never easy. Just as one group wants and values vulnerability and open honesty, the other group has impossible expectations about the pastor. This is probably an age issue, but not always. The other group wants the assurance that the pastor is the model of the spiritual life that it has deemed and judged appropriate. Of course, what this looks like from congregation to congregation is inconsistent, but it is always there. Whether it is how he preaches, how quickly he returns phone calls, how godly his kids are, or how involved his wife is, they expect him to be the model man in the congregation. Obviously, a man cannot meet both expectations without being dishonest to one group or being viewed as a failure by the other group.

A friend of mine described a personal experience with his church board. As the pastor, he was committed to being vulnerable and open in the pulpit so that he could relate to the problems of the congregation. His ministry grew, and people flocked to the church. But in one of the elders' meetings, the board scolded him for giving the congregation the impression that it's OK to have marriage problems, and that in sharing his marriage problems he was making some think he wasn't qualified for ministry.

I believe only the laity can address this tension. To do what needs to be done to reach and win men for the church, the leaders must figure out whether they want the appearance of perfection or honesty in their ministers. I think this will go a long way in helping men feel more comfortable in an uncomfortable place. One reason men don't feel comfortable in church is that they don't feel comfortable with ministers or the kind of life they model.

Unclear Game Plan

Another reason Sundays are uneasy for men is that they don't understand the game. Men appreciate having clear leadership and knowing the rules of the game being played. In their absence, every man must figure out what in the world the pastor is trying to do and what the church is all about. A minister needs at least three years of study to figure it out, and then he spends the rest of his life trying to implement it. The man off the street doesn't have a clue, especially if he is a convert late in life. One man told me when he first started attending the church, he thought the Epistles were the apostles' wives! I answered, "You mean they're not?" The church can be a very confusing place, and pastors are not very good at communicating their expectations.

In preparation for one of the Lausanne conferences on evangelism, Dallas businessman Ford Madison was asked to speak on the role of the layman in world evangelization. He surveyed various men who were actively involved in their churches to get a feel for what they thought their pastors really expected of them. He asked, "What do you think your pastor expects of you as a layman?" Ford said he was surprised by the results. The number one expectation was for men to give money. The number two perceived expectation was to attend and support all the church programs. The third, in Ford's words, was, "Don't rock the boat."[3]

What a sad commentary that the average man in the church cannot see beyond the offering and advertised programs to what the pastor really wants! I'm sure if the same question had been asked of the pastors, they would have responded, "Wanting men to grow in their relationship with Christ, to live a life glorifying to God, or to cultivate good family relationships." The problem is one of perception. Men perceive the church a certain way and then act in accordance with their perceptions. If the perceptions are off, their actions will be, too.

> Men perceive the church a certain way and then act in accordance with their perceptions. If the perceptions are off, their actions will be, too.

To bridge this gap, pastors need to better communicate their hearts to bring men to the center of what the church is all about. The men of the church need to recognize their main responsibility is not giving money or supporting programs but doing the ministry themselves. Once men see what the church is all about and have a personal share in its ministry, they feel at home there. They know what the bottom line is.

Richard Halverson, noted pastor and now chaplain of the United States Senate, said on one occasion to a group of pastors,

There are three kinds of church*men* I have seen. The first are the *church*men. These are those who live and work for the local church. They are faithful to the programs, give their money, fix the physical plant things, and make sure everything runs right. The second kind are the *worldly* churchmen. These come to church, give their token gifts, but they live for the world. The world of business, career, and personal goals. . . . The third are *world* churchmen. These are men who are in the church but who reach beyond the church to the world. They support the programs but they would rather be involved in personal ministry in the world. They are willing to teach Sunday school but their hearts are in small groups or leading a prayer group at the company. They see the concerns of God as what they can do about them in the world.[4]

I would add that the third kind are rare for a reason. Most men feel more comfortable doing the things at church related to the physical plant and finances. They perceive them as the more manly things. However, because these things need to be done in most churches, most pastors find it difficult to move men beyond them and explain the other, more-important-in-the-long-term goals. But I think if the clergy can clarify their goals for the church, men can turn their energies away from trying to figure them out on their own to deciding how to serve their church and their God.

There is a related issue. Some men who have been in the church don't want to go back. I'm not talking about skeptics, heretics, or those who have left because of church discipline. I'm talking about the men who have been faithful to the church programs, giving their money as an expression of their love for God, but have gotten burned or have burned out.

Many men in the church have been burned—burned by building programs or board meetings; burned by manipulation by pastors or their wives; burned by investing so much of their time, energy, and money into something that then turns around and retaliates. They are still in the church, but they are not excited to be there and they certainly don't feel comfortable.

Other men are burned out. The motto is, "I've done my time. Now let some of the newer or younger men serve." Dr. Howard Hendricks has told me on numerous occasions he sees this growing population within evangelicalism. Speaking at laymen's conferences and men's retreats around the country, he has noticed a missing age group—men over fifty. It is as if a whole group of churchmen have given up on the church. Not because they have conflicting beliefs or because they have been burned. They are just tired! They are still in the church, but they who were once in the fray of activity are now on the sidelines, watching the action.

Consider the typical scenario for a man. Let's say he has not had the benefit (or some would say liability) of being raised in the church, and he makes a personal decision through some high-school or college ministry. He marries, begins to have kids, and sees the need for his family to join a church. He seeks a church with age-graded classes for his kids, and his wife wants some activities for women. They find a full-service church and readily get involved. By the end of his thirtieth year, he is an adult class leader, and he and his wife hold a couples' Bible study in their home. Around age thirty-five, he has enough gray hairs to be considered a deacon. He is elected and begins to care for the needy in the church. At age forty, he is qualified to be an elder. He serves ten years as an elder, his kids are gone, and he and his wife think seriously about spending more time at the beach or the mountains. He has done his time. He played the church game; he did it well; but now at age fifty where else does he go? What else is there to this thing called Christianity?

I conclude he could have missed genuine, biblical ministry completely! We have so institutionalized the church today that it is hard for men to think in ministry terms unless they are ordered by *Robert's Rules of Order*. One man asked me, "Who was Robert anyway? Is he somewhere in the Bible?" We so faithfully ran our board meetings by him the fellow figured Robert must have been there with Moses or Peter!

One reason I am convinced men put up with so many irrelevant, pedantic discussions in church committee meetings (though they would never tolerate them in their own business) is that those are the only places they feel comfortable in the church. At least a board meeting, where men are gathered around a table discussing the business of the church, is a format they are familiar with. One elder told me that he has to pinch himself in the middle of some church meetings because they are no different from his company's meetings. Apart from opening in prayer or having a brief devotional, the meeting part is always the same.

A basic question needs to be raised: Is this the business of the church? I contend not. We cannot keep men involved in these meetings until they go to the grave. The meetings may drive them to an early grave, and we are not giving men a vision for what a lifetime of service is all about. The church is using and even abusing men's talents and time while refusing to build into them a love for God and a lifetime of service to their Master. Consequently, we are losing our most mature leaders because they are tired and there is nothing for them to do in the church that they haven't already done.

Until men look upon ministry as more than attending a meeting or making decisions, we will continue to lose the best men. In a little book he wrote in 1947, Elton Trueblood asked, "Why is it that the church is not getting the best men?" His question intrigued me, and his answer continues to haunt me. He replied, "Because they are the best men. . . . The best men are not interested in trivial things." His statement hurts deeply, but it contains a certain irony.

Christianity is no trivial pursuit. As C. S. Lewis concluded, if it is true we should not sleep at night. But the way Christianity is presented and lived out in the church, it is often reduced to the most insignificant trivia. It's no wonder men want no part in it. Men would rather risk their lives on the stock market, spend their time on the golf course, and find meaning in the profit-and-loss statement every month. If we do not call men to true Christianity and challenge them to invest their lives personally, not institutionally, I fear we will continue to lose the best men.

Recently, I met with such a man. Frank had done his church time and had gotten tired of the institutional game playing. For the past several years he had focused on small meetings with men at breakfast or lunch, meeting with them on their own turf, listening to them, praying with them, helping them sort out work options. I asked, "Where do men like you come from? Did the church give you a vision for what you are doing now and help you get started?" Unfortunately, he answered, "The church can't take the credit. My first job out of college, I was a new Christian trying to integrate my faith with business. Some older guys, for no apparent reason to me, took me under their wing to teach me the business and how to walk with Christ in the business world." Some people would think Frank had drastically pulled out of church leadership after becoming disillusioned with the church. In fact, he had given up institutional leadership for true personal ministry. There is a significant difference.

I have seen too many good men leave the church or church leadership because they were tired of playing the games and they saw a lot of what the church was doing as a waste of time. We must recapture the church for men, defeminize it, and make our appeals to men where it will cost them something more than their money or their time. *Christ wants their lives.*

Unresolved Father Issues

> *We must recapture the church for men, defeminize it, and make our appeals to men where it will cost them something more than their money or their time.*

As noted several times, father issues haunt our manhood, no matter where we are in the life span. Although many have wrestled with the question of extensive male absence from church, some have wondered if it may reflect our unresolved issues with our earthly fathers. After all, if God is our Father and the father message is not all that positive to me, my picture of the heavenly Father is not all that attractive.

In the context of this discussion some of the theological-psychological connections have fascinated me. As I travel to and speak in many different kinds of churches, I have noticed the kinds of churches that have greater representations of men. Almost uniformly, the churches with the most men are those in which men perceive the pastor as a strong leader. Also, I have found a tendency toward more control of behavior in the congregation and a view of God that stresses His holiness and sovereignty. Are men more attracted to an image of God that reminds them of their own distant, austere, and controlling fathers? I can't prove the observation, but it raises some interesting issues for discussion.

By the way, I can predict that the churches emphasizing a God of love, grace, mercy, and compassion will have more women than men. To a large extent, men consider these attributes weak. One psychologist (who asked not to be named) told me that from his experience in counseling, the more insecure the man, the more he will be into control issues and consequently the more Calvinistic in his theology. I don't like psychologizing about belief systems, but I have to admit I have reached similar conclusions.

> *If men are more attracted to churches where control, strong leadership, and a view of a transcendent and distant God are common, what does that mean?*

If men are more attracted to churches where control, strong leadership, and a view of a transcendent and distant God are common, what does that mean? Should we merely give men such a program to make them feel comfortable or perhaps address how our own developmental issues with our fathers have contributed to our perceptions of God and the church?

Having served in many Christian institutions and on several church staffs, I have concluded that a host of men have never really been affirmed as men by their fathers and, therefore, are largely incapable of expressing it to other men. They hide from vulnerable, caring relationships in their reports, organizational structures, policies, and standardized approaches to problems. Gordon Dalbey says, "This basic male urge to control relationships by rules has profound and indeed, ominous implications for the church, for it undermines the very heart of the gospel."[5] They are like their God—distant, in control, rigid, unemotionally "willing" the course of action. They are like their fathers.

Perhaps we need to say to men, "It's OK to be vulnerable. God is both in control and compassionate. Without His compassion, the whole world would be out of control!" Men may still deem this a weak message, but at least it is more healthy and, I believe, more theologically correct. Helping men resolve the real father issues with their human fathers may also be involved.

———— ■ ————

How do we reclaim men for the kingdom of God and get them into the doors of the church? I wish I knew a surefire answer. But two images come to my mind as I close this chapter. One is the image with which I started: the sterile, cold, formal, flowery image of church with over half its audience women. The other image is the most recent Flyers hockey game I experienced, and I mean experienced! I looked at the audience, by far more men than women. What were they wearing? Anything! Some were dressed for the stock exchange; others for the Philly meat market. How did they behave? Were they passive, quiet, unemotional, refined gentlemen? Hardly. They were involved, vocal, upset, yelling, celebrating. I thought to myself, *Here is a man's world, a place where he can let it all out, be himself, wear anything he desires, and they still let him in. And he actually pays to come!* But what about the church? No, there a man can't be himself; he has to watch what he says, act appropriately, and wear a neatly pressed and coordinated suit and tie. Then it hit me: *We're all dressed the way our mommies always wanted us to dress. We're all nice, clean little boys, sitting quietly so we won't get into trouble with our mothers!*

Am I suggesting we turn the church into a hockey game? Of course not. (After all, someone might get hurt.) But I do know that men will come to something and pay for it when we identify with it. It's obvious we don't feel that way about church, so I continue to think about the hockey game.

Maybe there's a way to make this thing called church more attractive to men and make our Sundays a little less uneasy. Perhaps if we could have our own private faith, one that really related to us and not the feminized version found in so many churches, our spiritual manhood could be easier. But here, too, it seems manhood issues are as uneasy as other areas. Even the spiritual pursuit is uneasy.

CHAPTER 9

Uneasy Spirituality

Or Why Men Always Feel Women Are More Spiritual

———— ■ ————

I was in a meeting with a group of women when they asked me what I was going to do to make the men "more spiritual." The women of the church had all kinds of Bible studies, various study groups, and a very well-thought-out approach to discipleship. After a little thought, I answered, "Well, I would like to put something together for the men, but I need your help." "Sure," they eagerly answered. "What do you want us to do?" I placed my tongue firmly in my proverbial cheek and responded, "I need you to work full-time and support your husbands so that they will be free during the daytime hours to do a discipleship program!" I don't think they liked my idea. But I made my point.

Let's face it, ladies. A lot of you have enjoyed your upper-middle-class luxury of free time. Oh, I know you think you are busy, but I also notice you have plenty of time for hair, nail, and tanning appointments, exercise classes, and the country club routine. For the Christian woman, there's an additional Christian list of a few Bible classes and prayer groups. I do not mean to criticize properly placed involvement, but I resent the unfair comparison with husbands and men in general. Now that many women are working outside the home again, some are beginning to appreciate the tension of trying to be a growing Christian while living in Babylon most of the week.

When men compare their lives to those of their wives, they believe they are not quite as spiritual because they just can't attend as many meetings. Consequently, they have a deep-seated inferiority complex about spiritual things. The issue here is what constitutes the standard for the Christian life. In most men's minds, the standard is whatever their wives are into, so that makes the standard feminine!

Men Don't Read

For the women who may be sheepishly reading this book, I'll let you in on some masculine "Christian secrets." The first is that most men don't read. I already mentioned that women read 80 percent of the Christian books. I don't have the stats available, but based on my interviews of men from many walks of life and levels of education, I would suggest the percentage is accurate. (Even I purchase a lot of books that I never read.)

You see, men basically don't read. I don't mean they *can't* read, although one would be surprised by how many successful men have reading problems. Bank presidents and military academy grads have confessed to me their basic difficulties in reading. The reason for their difficulty often lies back in their uneasy boyhood, as we discussed in chapter 1. They have a slower start at the gate and rarely recover from the feminine advantage. But the significant point here is that men don't read anything outside the field they work in.

I read Christian books, but that is my profession, my field

of work. My wife loves novels. My philosophy is, Why waste so much time on something that's not even true? That writes off the whole fiction category! Men read the *Wall Street Journal* and trade magazines if they are in business, or they may glance through *People* or *Field and Stream*. But they do not naturally pick up Calvin's *Institutes* or the Bible unless they are highly motivated or stuck in a pastor's home for a week without anything else to do.

That brings me to another part of this secret. When men read, they don't read for long periods of time. I have had little success in giving men books to read. I met with one man almost weekly. In the course of our breakfasts and lunches we would usually touch on some issues in his life that revealed some need or interest. I always went back to my pharmacy of books and pulled an appropriate prescription that I then dropped off at his house. Eventually, I realized I was moving my library to his house. I asked his wife, "Is Chuck reading all those books?" She looked at me, somewhat embarrassed, and said, "I really appreciate the time you spend with Chuck, but I don't think he has read any of the books you have dropped off. You see, he just doesn't read!"

From that point, I took a different approach. I copied one chapter of a book, highlighted the main points, and gave it to him to read. That worked far more successfully. Actually, I learned the technique in the air force watching how commanders operate with their staffs. It's almost a rule of thumb. The more stars officers have, the more they want to be briefed, and I mean brief. You had better be able to substantiate everything you say, but all they really want is the bottom line: "Are they for us or against us? Do you recommend him, or don't you? Are twenty-four birds [airplanes] mission capable, or is it twenty-five?"

Men will read something brief. That is why I write a devotional letter for men entitled the *Men's Memo*. It is very short, no more than ten lines triple-spaced (that's important), and I insist it be sent to their work address because that's where men read. I want to invade their normal reading time with something that will jog their minds back to the Lord and His Word for them as men. It has been very successful, with the added by-product that some of my most faithful readers are the secretaries who open the mail. One of these days I am going to write a similar letter for women.

That takes me to my third secret about men's reading habits. If you write for men, if it is short and it invades their reading time, they will read it if it is relevant. Because it is written for men, women also want to read it. I don't understand this phenomenon, but I know it's true. I received a hostile call from a woman who wanted a subscription to my *Men's Memo*. She was ready to label me a male chauvinist because I would write a devotional letter and distribute it only to men. I quickly disarmed her by saying I'd be glad to send her the letter. I then asked, "I'm curious. Do men have the freedom to buy *Mademoiselle?*" She answered, "Of course." "But do men buy *Mademoiselle* and actually read it rather than just look at some of the more revealing photos?" She finally admitted, "I guess they don't." Then she blurted out, "But I love looking through and reading *GQ!*"

I don't understand it, but there is another male-female difference. Write for men, and both men and women will read it. Write only for women, and only women will read it. That's why I'm writing for the men! Men feel inferior spiritually because they know they do not read as much as women do, and that makes their spiritual life uneasy. At the same time, because of their work schedules, they have fewer opportunities for biblical education than women have. In a *Leadership* article on men,[1] Bob Kroning notes, "Men keep wild schedules, and they don't want another thing to go to."

This last point raises a serious question about the whole Christian education process and spiritual maturity. What is the relationship between literacy and Christian maturity? Or to put it another way, is our goal literacy or learning? Often we are so culture-bound, we find it hard to think in any other categories except the American, Western world, upper-middle-class, educated values. One summer I taught a course in Cochabamba, Bolivia. Many students I taught had only a third-grade reading level (in Spanish); some could not read at all. For the first time in my life I had to face a new dimension about the entire Christian growth process. Can a man or a woman without the ability to read be a mature Christian? I must say, some of the most spiritually minded people I have ever met were some of the Bolivian mountain pastors. To answer my own question, yes, learning is the goal of or the means to Christian maturity, not literacy or reading ability. In Cochabamba I taught hungry hearts and inquiring minds.

> *Write for men, and both men and women will read it. Write only for women, and only women will read it.*

There are many ways to learn. I asked a naval academy graduate how he was able to get through such a rigorous academic environment with his "secret" reading difficulty. He simply said, "I listened well."

Men can learn through listening to cassette tapes. I know men who don't read well or much, but they listen to tapes when they jog, play golf, or drive the car. Some of these men can quote Chuck Swindoll, Jim Dobson, and Charles Stanley. They are learners, and if I understand what disciples are, that's what they are. If they are learning, there is no reason for these men to kick themselves around the house for not being as spiritual as their wives.

Men Don't Pray

A second secret is equally important: men don't pray. Oh, it's not that they don't want to pray or that they don't necessarily know how. It's just that prayer seems so . . . so . . . feminine! And why is that? Usually, the wife compares her husband's prayers (when he does pray with her) to what she thinks the standard of appropriate prayers should be—the pastor's.

As a former pastor, let me share (we can never just say something; we have to share it) with you some inside truth. At one point in my married life, Cinny, my wife, asked, "Why don't you pray at home with us the way you do in the pulpit?" My answer was short and simple: "Seminary taught me to pray that way. The way I really pray is the way I pray at home." I suggest that men pray the way they talk and women pray the way they talk. There is a connection between our brains and our mouths, even when we pray. At least I hope there is!

Our prayer time had stimulated Cinny's question. Cinny and I had listed our prayer requests: things for the kids, some church needs, some issues we were facing. Then we prayed. She prayed her way, lengthy, with lots of words, reminders, and explanations. Then I prayed, "Lord, we need some money, control Graham at school, give Charis a friend at school, and deal with the situation at church. Amen!" Cinny looked at me and said, "Is that it?" "Sure," I responded. "Didn't we cover everything?" She came back, "But I thought we would pray a little longer. You pray so beautifully in the pulpit. Why don't you pray like that here?"

Now I try to pray differently . . . that's right, in church. I believe I please the Lord more by being honest and not so flowery. And I provide a better model for all the men who feel guilty because they don't know what *providence* or *sovereignty* means because they didn't go to seminary. Somehow I think the women still like the flowery prayers better, though. They feel more reassured by the length and theological passion. I would rather pray as a man when I pray, and not for any particular group.

We men pray like we talk, which means we pray with few words and to make the point. I am convinced the Lord is not necessarily pleased by our lengthy explanations or use of theological terms. He is our Father, and He knows what's in our hearts.

Men should never feel inferior because they pray differently from their wives. The essential point is that they pray. That's the only question I ask men. When I asked one man about his prayer life, he said, "Yes, I pray every morning on the way to work. I turn the radio off, commit my day to Him, and pray for my wife and kids." I asked, "Have you ever told your wife that?" "No," he said. "I figured it wouldn't really count with her since she goes to all those prayer meetings." I want you to know I came unglued in front of that man! He prayed every day for his family on the way to work, but he held his prayer life in disregard because it didn't measure up to his wife's expectations. That takes me to my next secret.

Feelings of Incompetency

Men gravitate toward their competencies and flee from their weaknesses. A common question women ask me about their husbands is, "Why won't they take more leadership at home?" I in turn ask, "Where do they spend their time?" "At work," they reply. "Why?" I ask. "They love work!" No, I don't think men love work all that much, but they feel competent at work. They don't feel competent at home, that is, in spiritual nurturing skills. I still don't, despite much theological and educational study in the field.

One man told me of his discomfort in leading family devotions. He said he had not come from a Christian home and did not have a model of a father who had done such things. At work we usually give adequate training to make persons feel competent in their tasks, but apparently this is not the case in the church. Finally, I asked him, "Could you take your son [age three], put him on your lap after dinner, and just read him something?" He said, "Sure." Then he asked, "What should I read to him?" "That's probably irrelevant right now, just the feel of sitting on his father's lap and hearing his father's voice will produce more good feelings than any of the best content."

He seemed liberated. I believe he had the Norman Rockwell view of family devotions—the perfect family seated at the dinner table, with all eyes fixed on dad while he read from the family (King James, of course) Bible. From two-year-olds to teens, all are transfixed on father's masterful enunciation and enthusiasm for the biblical text.

If that's the model, it's no wonder men feel so out of it. No one has families like that anymore (if such families ever existed). More true to reality is this scene: the two-year-old has just spilled his milk all over the family Bible, and the teenager sits there with arms folded, smirking and finally responding by saying, "This is boring. Can we go yet?" A father who does anything of a spiritual nature with his kids is way ahead of the pack in terms of our culture. This man should be celebrated as a rare breed and exalted for his attempts rather than castigated by an endless list of pseudospiritual expectations.

Male Spirituality

> *A father who does anything of a spiritual nature with his kids is way ahead of the pack in terms of our culture.*

Men have their own unique spirituality. If their brains work differently, their tongues speak differently, they work and experience their relationships differently, their spiritual approach will also be unique. Their masculine uniqueness will color their tastes and needs in the realm of spiritual pursuits as well. Spiritual programs, guides, and materials that minister to women may not necessarily minister to men. The failure to observe this distinction and have it affect church programming and approaches makes for one more uneasy experience of manhood.

It's time to affirm that our spiritual needs as men are not the same as those of women. This is not to say that one is more right than the other. But it is to say that there is a critical need to understand and make allowances for the male perspective and appreciate his unique contributions and approaches to the Christian life. The Christian life and spiritual formation have not for some time been considered manly. When the women's revolution began, many of our sisters in the faith criticized the long-standing traditions of spirituality as being male-dominated, ignoring the needs and contributions of women. They usually referred to the well-known spiritual mystics, reformers, and theologians who were men.

Our response was to encourage them to get the same education, learn Hebrew and Greek, join the theologue club, and develop feminine theologies. Many did, even though I think their primary focus has been on getting feminine pronouns used in reference to God rather than doing the harder task of developing well-integrated theological works.

I believe we, as men, have been greatly helped by their distinctive contributions. However, the comparison between where women are today and where men were in the Middle Ages is perhaps an improper comparison. The men of those centuries were not the kind of laymen who now fill our churches. They were priests, professors, missionaries, full-time workers, the standard models of the spiritual life.

I believe the masculine models needed today for male spirituality are more like C. S. Lewis, Malcolm Muggeridge, Chuck Colson, Alexander Solzhenitsyn, Czechoslovak President Vaclav Havel, and a host of other committed laymen living in the obscurity of an ungodly world. But they live for Christ and try their best to somehow make a difference where they are. I believe this is true spirituality. It is not an isolated-in-a-cave spirituality but a spirituality for the real world. Although it will never be easy, at least it will be more realistic than the one often professed to be so spiritual based on ancient history.

Because most men I know have not had the time to read ancient history and sort out the various approaches to the spiritual life, I have tried to provide a simplified overview here. Men seem to fall into spiritual habits that may or may not be constructive to their spiritual lives. I have attempted to give them the range of historical practices so that they can decide where they fit in.

Approaches to Spiritual Development

Animism

The oldest and most primitive approach to the spiritual world is that of animism. Most primitive societies practiced it, and it continues to be a part of many Third World cultures. The approach involves the belief that spirits indwell everything and that there are good spirits and evil spirits. Animism makes very little distinction between the material and the spiritual worlds. Rocks, trees, and lakes can be inhabited by certain spirits. I'm sure most men reading this would say, "That's far-out stuff. I would never accept that." However, the remark shows how little thinking we as men sometimes give to the most casually accepted Christian practices.

A group of men once asked me what I thought about Ouija boards. It was Halloween, and a teacher at school had the kids play the game. Boy, did I get into a heated debate! I don't think school time should be wasted by playing with Ouija boards; they have no place in school. But I replied, "Do you think that every one of these games put out by the manufacturers is indwelled by an evil spirit?" Most answered, "Yes." I responded, "So you are saying that somewhere in the process of making this game, a spirit is assigned to each game and given the job of deceiving and making each kid believe in Satan's power?" I could take this further, but I won't.

Is there any relationship between belief and indwelling? Do rocks have evil spirits in them by virtue of their being rocks? Or did a witch or priest have something to do with it? I don't believe something can be indwelled with evil qualities until someone desires it and becomes open to it. The game is a game until someone present calls upon Lucifer or the spirits to indwell the game. The question raises serious issues about demonology and how evil relates to this material world. The view often perpetuated as normal parental concern is really a subtle form of animism. My final point to men is that if a demon can indwell a Ouija board, he can indwell the stock market or my boat on the lake as well!

Eastern Mysticism

It's now in vogue to read New Age literature and hang crystals on your car's rearview mirror. Go into any shopping mall bookstore and look at the whole category of books under the New Age sign. It didn't even exist as a separate category ten years ago. The New Age is an Americanized version of Eastern mysticism with a little pop psych thrown in, neatly packaged and marketed by enlightened superstars.

The fundamental belief of Eastern thought is that all reality is unified or one. Think of it as a river flowing somewhere and we are all in the river as one little drop of water. Therefore, the key is finding the flow and going with it.

The goal is enlightenment, which comes by turning within oneself and looking for something of the divine spark. In this thought, material and spiritual are fused and largely indistinguishable. We find the divine by finding ourselves and establishing some union with whatever we find within. When we find it, we have become enlightened. I asked a Hare Krishna once what enlightenment was. He answered, "Enlightenment is one hand clapping." That's Eastern thought.

Many Christians attack this New Age philosophy whenever possible. Historically, it has been in our own camp, however. Some of the greatest Christian mystics during the Middle Ages sought an experiential union with God. The processes and meditations they describe are very close to language I have read in New Age literature. Those mystics wrote many of our

Christian classics during times of serious seeking of the divine within, times when they fasted, prayed, and meditated. Even some current discussions about the inner self or the inner child bear similarity to Eastern thought. Freud's view of the unconscious mind, which has never really been proved, also has certain similarities to seeing another self within the self on the outside.

I don't see men flocking to the New Age category in bookstores, probably because they are not as introspective as women. But I wanted to reveal that men face this current approach to the spiritual life in many different forms.

Greek Philosophy

One of my theology professors opened class by saying, "Have we really ever moved beyond the Greeks?" His implied answer was, "No, we haven't." We don't think about the Greek philosophers when we discuss spirituality. But often we use the very words and concepts that originated with them. As men, we have accepted a common Greek perception of the Christian life, thinking that it is right or biblical while not realizing its source.

Both Aristotle and Plato understood the importance of spiritual process without giving any clear reference to the role the gods or one God played in it. The pioneers of Greek thought said that spiritual development begins with a human spiritual craving, which leads the individual to pursue a change in his behavior. The change involves the avoidance and/or denial of nonspiritual impulses. The goal is *gnosis*, the Greek word for "knowledge." However, this knowledge is not knowledge as an intellectual pursuit; it is knowledge in the sense of "mysteries." In the pursuit of the spirit (human), one is to encounter the divine mysteries.

Aristotle emphasized the role of the intellect and reason in the process, whereas Plato saw the necessity of denying the material impulses, which only short-circuit spiritual development. In time, Greek thought became Gnosticism, which made a distinct separation between the material and the spiritual worlds; matter was evil, and the things of the spirit were good. Therefore, the goal of spiritual development was cultivating the human spirit while restraining the evil impulses of the material world.

Every time I teach on this subject, I love to watch the faces of the people in the class. Occasionally, one extrovert will blurt out, "That's what I was raised on in my church." Yes, there's a lot of Greek Gnosticism in the church being offered in the guise of biblical spirituality. Some Aristotelian rationalists think that by believing the right things, spiritual development will happen, so they emphasize teaching and believing right doctrine. The Platonists (legalists) believe that the things of the material world are evil and, therefore, should be avoided to be a growing Christian. The spiritual life is then focused on denying the ungodly impulses, which only corrupt the human and divine spirit. This makes for a fairly easy-to-understand spirituality (which explains why so many men lean that way), but I have serious doubts whether these processes lead to a genuine encounter with the living God.

Jewish Spirituality

Jewish spirituality is hard to classify since Judaism is broken into three different camps: Orthodox, Conservative, and Reform.[2] Add the Hasidic and Cabalistic branches, and a wide variety of spiritual approaches is taught. But historically, some beliefs are uniform. The overarching concern of spiritual life seems to be reestablishing the covenant relationship between God and His people as it once was. Therefore, a fundamental look back into history as the covenant people is balanced by a current desire to have this covenant relationship restored to more biblically based practices (freedom to practice religion, build a temple, and reinstitute Levitical laws). Others believe that the spiritual life centers on God's presence among His people, in the Torah, and in the living community. Traditionally, the spiritual approach also expressed the yearning for the day of completion when God's presence will be more universally known. Some believe this to be the messianic hope. The more mystical groups regard all spiritual experiences here and now as foretastes of the messianic age.[3]

Certainly, Christian spirituality has much of its origin in these Jewish concepts. They are not original with Jesus or the apostles. We value the sense of redemptive history because we share the Hebrew Bible with our Jewish friends. We see their history as our history, and we believe that history is not only important but also true and foundational for everything else we believe. If God has not spoken and acted in history, our faith and spiritual development mean nothing.

While I was in seminary, an Indian student was getting ready to go back to his country during the summer. I asked him, "Why don't you schedule your flight so you can have a layover in Israel?" He looked puzzled and finally answered, "Why would I want to do that?" My brother was a Christian in the faith, but he still had a Hindu-Indian view of nonhistory. It didn't matter whether the events of the Bible happened or not; it really wasn't a part of his faith in Jesus. He could see no connection between his faith and the history of Israel.

The flip side of this happened in Israel. I was sitting at a cafe when a tour bus stopped right in front of me and began off-loading its passengers. The tour was obviously arranged for American Jews. One woman asked if she could sit at my table. Her first comment to me was, "Whew, seeing all this stuff almost makes you think it really happened!" She was on her way to discovering her faith.

The Christian view of spirituality also shares the belief of the covenant people. We believe that the blood of the Messiah, Jesus, has ratified an entirely new covenant, which was promised originally to the Jewish community but has in these last days been graciously given to us as Gentiles (Jer. 31:31; Luke 22:20). That does not mean Jews cannot share in it, but Gentiles have been given access by God to be cosharers in this

"Jewish covenant." This covenant relation through Jesus is also foundational to our spiritual development.

We share a view of the future with this Jewish spirituality. We believe that history is going someplace and that this is not the best of all possible worlds. We believe that history will be consummated not by man's entering us into a kingdom on earth but by a supernatural divine invasion from without. We share a belief in the coming of our Messiah, when all our dreams and desires will be fulfilled.

Before we go any further, I want to look at three male tendencies. To argue for a distinct male spirituality, we must first come to grips with how much of our approach is determined by our personality, background, and experiences. I see this in myself and in many men I work with. We do not recognize why we believe as we do or why we favor one tradition over another. More often than not, our approach to the spiritual life is a mere extension of ourselves.

Understanding Our Inhibitors

> *To argue for a distinct male spirituality, we must first come to grips with how much of our approach is determined by our personality, background, and experiences.*

Most men don't talk about epistemology. Epistemology concerns the science of knowing; it gets at how we know what we know. I had never heard the term until I went to seminary, and frankly, I've never heard it used since then in everyday conversation. Yet, in many ways, this science ought to be taught as one of the first sciences.

We devote little time to trying to evaluate claims to know something. We watch television ads and believe their claims without investigating their truthfulness or asking, "I wonder how they know that?" Most of us take leaps of faith each day on what we believe. But there is usually some connection as to why we believe as we do and reasons why we don't believe other things. This becomes vitally important in the spiritual life. These reasons determine our assumptions, our beliefs, our direction and approaches.

Over the past twenty years of working with men, my toughest task has been getting them to look at why they do what they do and believe what they do. Being the rational creatures that we are, we would like to believe that all our convictions have been carefully thought out and contrasted against erroneous views. The truth is, we haven't done that. What we believe is probably more a reflection of who we are, where we have been, and what has happened to us. In this section, we are really talking about the influences on our thinking, believing, and acting in the spiritual realm.

Role of Personality

I don't know how many hours I have spent in committee and board meetings, but it seems like half my life. (I don't like them. Is it obvious?) In each meeting the same people seem to show up. There are what some have called the thinkers, feelers, doers, and sleepers (ones who never say anything).[4] My own categories are leaders, bean counters, emoters, deviants, clowns, healers, and Mr. Nice guys. I've seen them in every group I've been in. They show up as if they have been assigned to the group (I won't tell you which I am). If I could group these in two categories related to the spiritual life, I would group them as rational doers and intuitive artists. These are the two standard approaches based on personality that I have observed.

A good example of the rational doer is the engineer or the financial bean counter who brings to the spiritual life a mind desiring order and precision, who likes rules, definitions, clarity, and smooth-running organization. These are great qualities, but the real question is whether or not he should seek to build an entire spiritual life around them. A more important question is whether or not he should expect others to conform to these attributes when they are so clearly right to him. They seem right because they are extensions of his psychological view of life.

In the spiritual realm, this man likes order in his Christian life, regular devotions, strict tithing, a church that is smooth running and has a solid bottom line. He is suspicious of those who are freewheeling, sensitive, and disordered, and who give "as the Spirit leads." My estimation is that he hinders his own growth and development in the spiritual realm as long as he views the Christian life entirely through his personality grid and does not allow himself (or others) to grow beyond it.

At the other extreme of the personality spectrum is the intuitive artist. (I am purposefully presenting these types as extremes. I realize that most men are combinations, with varying degrees of one or the other. However, I believe most men are dominant in one of them.) The artist does not oppose order and rule, but his heart beats for other things. He goes with the intuitive feel of things; he likes spontaneity and the relational aspect of things. He appreciates life's subtleties, and ambiguities don't confuse him. Obviously, this man can be attracted to a view of the spiritual life that is a mere extension of his personality grid. He likes to commune with God; he enjoys the mystical elements of faith; he likes to experience the biblical truths. Church architecture, look, and smell—all are important elements for his worship.

As can be expected, these two men do not see the world of faith the same way. Will they realize that their faith is similar to their personalities and grant the value of other expressions? I believe the failure to recognize this aspect and embrace it is the reason for many church splits and extreme conflicts. I also believe God would have us move beyond our personalities and see the spiritual life in broader and more novel terms. He is an infinite God. No two personalities are alike, so there should be a variety of spiritual expressions, all equal and valued in the kingdom. Basing a whole religious expression on my personality is a serious act of idol worship; my personality becomes the god to be worshiped. But another hindrance has become another god to be worshiped.

Role of Background

- "Why can't we sing more of the older hymns of the faith?"
- "Shouldn't our ministers wear robes? They would cover up their cheap suits with uncoordinated ties."
- "It's not really Sunday unless you go to both morning and evening services."
- "People shouldn't talk after entering the sanctuary. Silence is more glorifying to God."
- "Make a joyful noise to the Lord. Don't just sit there quietly."
- "Why does this church have two pulpits when my other church had one?"
- "That was real wine in the Communion cups today."
- "The sermon was too long."
- "We need more time for prayer during the service."
- "I don't think there should be announcements once the service begins."

No two personalities are alike, so there should be a variety of spiritual expressions, all equal and valued in the kingdom.

All these statements and questions illustrate the power and strength of one's background to affect his present approach to the spiritual life. A pastor trying to put remarks like these together in one service has an impossible task. A man must realize the source of such statements before he can take his spiritual journey seriously.

He can make two responses to his background, both of which can seriously hinder his growth and development.

The first is being bound to his background. Since he was raised Catholic, he'll die Catholic; or since he enjoyed the Sunday evening service while growing up, he now wants it in his church experience. It's almost beside the point to evaluate whether the times have changed or what it was about the service that he liked. The person will feel better just to have one for his spiritual development. I've seen men in church meetings argue passionately for such things—not realizing the basis for their belief. One man tried to argue that we should have Sunday night service because the whole day is the Lord's day.

The other background hindrance results from a negative or bad experience in the past, which determines spiritual life approaches in the present. A man may have been burned by one group, denomination, or church, and he vowed never to have the experience repeated. I've seen Jewish males become Catholic because of the way a rabbi treated them. I've seen Catholic men become Baptists because of their experience in parochial schools, and I've seen strict fundamentalists become emotional charismatics because of the legalistic, oppressive atmosphere they were raised in. When people have been hurt or disillusioned by some spiritual experience, they tend to go to another extreme; they can no longer see any value in the tradition from which they have come.

After I spoke to a group, a man came up to me and stated, "I was deeply offended by what you said about the Catholic priests." I had used an illustration from my days as an air force chaplain; I was pleasantly surprised at getting to know many priests, the ones I knew deeply loved Christ and His Word. My comments had offended this brother. Can you guess why? Yes, he was a former disgruntled Catholic who could not value or see spiritual life anywhere in Catholicism. To grow spiritually, we need to move beyond our background experiences— whatever they may have been.

A third hindrance involves experiences in adulthood. Most of our critical development occurs during childhood and adolescence, but often our adult exposure to life gives us many attitudes that may or may not benefit our growth spiritually. I know born-again Christians who were adult members in what they call liberal mainline denominations. Once they have a personal relationship with Christ, they react toward their church and the whole denomination. Again, they can see nothing of value in it. I've become aware of two kinds of "liberals": liberals by conviction (which are few), and liberals by education. In other words, they embraced the belief system of their school. Don't we all do that?

Some have been exposed to the older fundamentalism, which had its lists of do's and don'ts. Those churches were strong on evangelism, missions, and decisions for Christ. But they were also anticulture, anti-Communist, antiliberal, and largely anti-Democrat. Men may leave these churches and lose all regard for them. The reaction could also turn them against experiencing the person of Christ, valuing the Scriptures, and reaching others with the gospel.

I've also met those who have been burned by the Reformed faith. The Reformed faith is debated among its own adherents as to when one is reformed enough. But certainly it emphasizes the sovereignty of God, sovereign grace, the five points of Calvinism, and one's ordering of the eternal decree(s) of God (a which-comes-first discussion involving election, the death of Christ, the work of the Holy Spirit, repentance, and faith). One man told me that he got tired of the cold, abstract, doctrinal approach and became an Episcopalian. I hope he doesn't overreact and devalue the biblical doctrines of grace and sovereignty, which are critical to spiritual development.

Then there are the charismatics. This renewal movement, which began in the sixties during the Jesus movement, has gained tremendous inroads into almost all major denominations. It brought a unique, special contact with the Spirit, an openness to the miraculous, and a certain expectancy for God to work. Healing and speaking in tongues as spiritual experiences were viewed as normative for the devout.

But some people were turned off by the extremes, the fancy superstar and well-paid pastors and evangelists, and finally the moral lapses of leaders that have been so well publicized. Many weren't healed, and some admitted that they faked the tongues speaking experience to be included in the fold. They have been burned, and they are not about to have anything that smacks of "charismania" in their present spiritual experience.

That is unfortunate. In my last church, some members didn't like our singing choruses instead of the older hymns. Their reason: "They are charismatic songs." I guess they didn't realize that some of those older hymns were Methodist (Wesley) and Lutheran and even some were put to barroom tunes ("A Mighty Fortress Is Our God").

> *Before we can genuinely grow up as men in the spiritual life, we need to see where we have been hurt, where we are still bound, or how our personality is determining our approach to God.*

It's unfortunate that any time we overreact to a negative experience, we can no longer find any good thing in the experience. Before we can genuinely grow up as men in the spiritual life, we need to see where we have been hurt, where we are still bound, or how our personality is determining our approach to God. These areas must be identified, cleaned up, and cleared out before we can see what male spirituality can look like.

Aspects of Spiritual Development

One popular book on men's issues has a closing chapter on how to change or grow as a Christian man. The writer encourages Bible reading, witnessing, and confessing sin, all of which are important. We all know men who do these things, but apparently they don't bring about change or growth. Perhaps this thing called spiritual growth is more complex, if not mysterious.

I suggest that eight basic aspects must be considered to be a spiritually minded person, but none by itself will guarantee spiritual growth. I will center my thoughts on two metaphors, which I believe to be the long-standing pictures of what the spiritual life is all about.

The first metaphor is that of agricultural growth and development. Spiritual development is likened to the natural agricultural processes that God has built into the creation (Gen. 8:22). Jesus uses this image in describing how the Word of God grows in someone's heart. The point often misunderstood is that Jesus says that men will never know how the seed really grows! The gospel of Mark records Jesus' words: "The kingdom of God is as if a man should scatter seed on the ground, and should sleep by night and rise by day, and the seed should sprout and grow, he himself does not know how" (Mark 4:26–27).

The apostle Paul probably has more to say on the subject of spiritual growth than any other New Testament writer; yet, even he admits that this process has its own mystery. He writes to one of his churches, "Who then is Paul, and who is Apollos, but ministers through whom you believed, as the Lord gave to each one? I planted, Apollos watered, but God gave the increase" (1 Cor. 3:5–6). He admits the most any human can do to facilitate the growth of another is to cooperate with the natural (supernatural) processes that God has built into the spiritual word. Humans do not cause growth; only God does!

God has built certain properties into the spiritual seed to cause it to do what it was created to do when other conditions are right (loose soil, water, fertilizer, sun, and air). If we can push the analogy, all we can do as spiritually minded people is to make sure the proper conditions for growth exist. However, the actual growth process is ultimately a mystery. Even Jesus calls it so. That is why I don't accept simple formulas for growth and change when we are talking about the complexity of human development under the ministry of the Spirit.

But this concept does not sell well in a technological age when supposedly everything must be understood and reduced down to finding the right program to derive a desired result. Human beings are not computers. Their growth is better likened to an agricultural metaphor than a technological or business metaphor. However, because we don't like mystery and things we can't adequately explain, we go to other illustrations to help us understand the phenomenon. In the process we change the nature of what spiritual growth involves.

The other long-standing metaphor for spiritual growth is that of a pilgrimage. The spiritual life is a journey. This is the major theme in the wilderness experience of the people of God under the leadership of Moses, which is used as a model of pilgrimage in the New Testament (Exod. 13:17, 21; 1 Cor. 10:1-11). Jesus called His disciples to follow Him, which teaches the journey motif (Matt. 4:19-20). Being followers is the essence of discipleship for His first recruits. In regard to the doctrine of sanctification, Paul looks upon it as a progressive development over time, which also implies movement and journey (1 Cor. 1:2; 2 Cor. 7:1; 1 Thess. 5:23). The writer of Hebrews uses the imagery of a journey throughout his epistle (Heb. 6:1; 10:39; 11:10; 12:1; 13:14).

I find this picture very useful for helping men understand their struggles in the spiritual life. Many have come from backgrounds that teach salvation and sanctification as an instantaneous event, which should create immediate change within. This may be true for some. But the question I frequently hear is, "Why is it taking me so long to get better?" If spiritual life is viewed as life-changing events and commitments, there will be much disappointment and perhaps doubt about whether God is doing anything at all. But once the concept of journey is grasped, the expectations change. Each person's journey is different. My wife and I never take the same route to the same destination. She has her way, and I have mine!

Once we embrace the journey concept, all the other aspects of spiritual life can be understood in relationship to it. What, then, are the elements of this spiritual journey?

Time

A fundamental aspect of traveling is time. It takes time to get where we are going. We can try to reduce the amount of time by speeding or taking a faster form of transportation, but it will still take time to get where we want to be. So it is with the spiritual life. This basic element is often overlooked. The New Testament writers do not make a major issue of it; yet, they assume it throughout. Paul expected the Corinthians to be farther down the road in their spiritual experience because a certain amount of time had elapsed (1 Cor. 3:1–3). The writer to the Hebrews had the same expectation; he felt enough time had passed that they should be teaching others, but they weren't (Heb. 5:12).

Men need to be encouraged that no matter where they are on their spiritual journey, they aren't home yet. They are still en route. The only real question is, Are they stuck in some ditch, or have they turned around and headed back the other direction? By the way, this view of the spiritual life means that when they do get stuck in the ditch of sin or failure, they haven't suddenly been transported back to the original starting point. No matter how badly a man may have failed, I don't believe he goes back to zero to have to start all over again. That's what genuine confession is all about (1 John 1:9).

Truth

Time alone does not get us where we are going. The old pilot illustration is certainly true: "We have some good news and bad news for you. The good news is that we are making great time. The bad news is that we are lost." So it is with our life in the Spirit. We need a map. My wife likes to get the AAA "trip tiks" so that she can see the trip reveal itself progressively. I like to get one big map so I can see the whole trip. We both need a map to get where we are going.

That takes us back to our earlier epistemology question about how we know what we know. I don't like being called a Bible thumper or "one of those fundamentalists." Rather than defend my beliefs, I usually ask the antagonist what he bases his beliefs on. After some hemming and hawing, he'll usually admit that he has none or that they are based entirely on his personal opinion. At that point I ask whether he desires to rest his eternal destiny on his personal opinion. This approach presents the Bible in a different light.

The Bible is our map. Written by many authors over a one-thousand-year period of history, it provides illumination and information for our journey of life. It consistently claims to be the very word from God (Ps. 119:105–7; 2 Tim. 3:16; Rev. 22:18–19). Not to take that claim seriously is to disregard the best map provided for mankind. As Mark Twain said, "It's not what I don't understand in the Bible that bothers me; it is what I do understand!"

A man got caught in a buyout, and as president, the new company gave him one year to find other work for himself, but his main responsibility was to fire five hundred employees. When I went into his office overlooking center-city Philadelphia, there was an open, worn-out Bible on his desk.[5] I asked him, "What do you do with this?" He answered, "I feel like a pastor here. After putting an entire home in trauma, I try to give some spiritual resources to help deal with the loss of work they are facing." He understood the journey concept. People need an accurate map of truth to get them through difficult times and on to the next turn in life.

A Trustworthy Guide

The map of the Scriptures provides an objective source for direction on our journey. We need a trustworthy friend or guide who knows the territory and perhaps has been where we are going so he knows exactly how to get there. Many times we have asked for directions, and the response has been, "You can't get there from here" or "I haven't got a clue!"

We need someone who sticks with us and helps us on our journey as a personal guide. I don't claim to thoroughly understand the concept of the Trinity. But I do understand that these three persons of the Godhead are involved in our journey. God the Father has planned our trip (Rom. 8:28–30). God the Son has been before us on the same trip and knows where the rough spots are and how to get around them, and He has placed us on the same road (John 17:13–18). So that we would not feel abandoned by Him, He has sent into the world His own Spirit (John 15:26) who will be our personal guide and will be with us forever (John 16:13). This is the subjective personal reality that we have and need on our trip. No matter what happens on our journey, we have the promise that we are not alone. God Himself is very much involved in our lives.

Many times this reality has not seemed true to me. Even as I write this section, I write it by faith. My wife and I have been through difficulties that seemed to have no reason. We felt God was leading a certain direction and made decisions based on that, but the results were disastrous. What can we conclude from these experiences? We can conclude that God wasn't involved and somehow we missed His will or that maybe the Deists were right in thinking God doesn't really involve Himself in the affairs of men. Or we can consider what happened a part of our journey, and perhaps someday as we look back down the road, we can see why our lives took the turn they did.

As one of my theology professors said, "God's will is what *happened*. That's as far as I can take it." This is another part of the mystery. I want God to reveal Himself to me in ways I can recognize and understand, but often His silent presence is somehow mysteriously guiding me through this maze called life.

Trust

Trusting a guide takes faith. When we stop and ask directions, we put ourselves in the position of either believing the directions or not believing them. We can believe that we know better how to get where we are going, or we can merely trust our helper's guidance. As men, we trust in many things every day; yet, when it comes to the spiritual life, faith seems very uneasy. The uneasiness of faith makes for an uneasy manhood.

One psychotherapist alludes to his conversation with an older mentor in the process of his training. His mentor asked him, "Have you ever noticed what most men who need help have in common?" He says the answer surprised him coming from a therapist: "More often than not, men suffer from problems of faith."[6] The writer goes on to point out that men's crisis of faith also manifests itself in disbelief in themselves and everything else. Faith in oneself and the world has connections to faith in God.

There may be many reasons why it is so difficult for the most religious men to exercise faith. But one reason concerns control. One of our distinctive approaches to life as men is that we very much want to be in control. Our ego orientation begins with ourselves and moves outward into our environment; women's ego orientation begins with their environment and then moves in toward themselves.[7] When we men move into the larger environment, we desire to feel safe, and safety is found in controlling the environment.

On a trip after I realize I have taken a wrong turn, I must face the reality that I am lost. Being lost means I have lost control of my environment and I no longer feel safe. Asking directions places me in the position of having to trust someone else, and I don't like that. It makes me uncomfortable.

In the final analysis, faith is relinquishing control of my life or relinquishing whatever I am facing. True faith always begins in recognizing my seeking to control the situation by my own abilities but failing. I must then take the leap and trust someone else. Putting my trust in another develops me spiritually and humanly. David Heller observes, "Faith also enhances masculinity by helping a man determine his powerlessness."[8]

As one who has been in some kind of Christian work for over twenty years, I have often learned that those who appear faithful may not be truly faithful at all. This is not a condemnation, only an observation of my life and the lives of other men. I can mouth the fact that I am trusting God, but in trying to control everything—from what my family does to what happens in critical meetings at work or church—I demonstrate that I really don't want to give up control over others and hand it over to my heavenly Father. I have discovered that persons who operate under the guise of being responsible for everything that happens in the church are obsessive, controlling people. They have the freedom to be the way they are, but let's not hold them up as examples of faith. Faith is relinquishing control and trusting in something one cannot see (Heb. 11:1). The writer of Hebrews says, "Without faith it is impossible to please God." Control doesn't please God. Faith does!

Tension

The subject of faith brings us to the next reality of the difficulties we face along the way. During my childhood, my father always rose very early in the morning in preparation for starting our family vacations. As a pilot, he applied all of his preflight planning to auto trips as well. Next to all the suitcases in the trunk was his box of tools, suitable for doing anything to a car, including pulling the engine and replacing it with another. Dad was prepared. I didn't learn very well. I just take off, and when something breaks, I wonder why I didn't bring tape or something! My dad recognized that one should expect some things to go wrong on a journey. Tires blow; fuel pumps fail; roads are torn up; and detours must be taken. Each event creates tension within us.

The role of tension in the spiritual experience is often ignored or misunderstood. Some persons teach that if God is on your side, your path will be free of obstacles. The health-and-wealth gospel certainly does not value tension's role in the development of the spiritual life. In fact, the presence of tension is believed to demonstrate one's lack of faith or spirituality.

A few years ago, I wanted to read the entire New Testament to see what I could find on the subject of spiritual maturity and how to develop it. I could find only one clear passage where the concepts of spiritual maturity and something that produced it were found. The passage was in the epistle of James, written by the half brother of Jesus. James must have been a realist. He wrote, "Consider it all joy, my brethren, when you encounter various trials, knowing that the testing of your faith produces endurance. And let endurance have its perfect [mature] result that you may be perfect and complete, lacking in nothing" (James 1:2–4, NASB).

It is clear that trials place our faith under tension and develop us to maturity. That is why we should welcome trials as friends. I must confess this is not my usual posture when things happen on my journey. I'm usually angry, trying to figure out what I did wrong to deserve such treatment. But I can either accept the event by faith and trust it with my heavenly Father or allow it to consume me with anger and resentment. These wrong reactions can very easily lead to many dark nights of the soul. Anyone who has been stuck in a ditch through a dark, cold night on a lonely highway knows what I'm talking about. A few brothers have also experienced the dark nights of the spiritual soul.

Temptation

Our Lord told us to pray, "Do not lead us into temptation" (Matt. 6:13). Yet, His brother assumed temptation would come and said, "Let no one say when he is tempted, 'I am tempted by God.' . . . but each one is tempted when he is drawn away by his own desires and enticed" (James 1:13–14). The apostle Paul promised, "No temptation has overtaken you except such as is common to man; but God is faithful, who will not allow you to be tempted beyond what you are able" (1 Cor. 10:13).

Even though we pray that temptation will not come upon us, it probably will. But when it does, we can't blame God for it; we must bear the blame. However, the good news is that somehow God is involved in it, supervising it and limiting its duration and intensity.

In my spiritual development I can't think of anyone who clearly articulated how temptations relate to my spiritual growth. The teaching I've had always stops short by saying, "Don't give in to temptation." The reality is that we constantly do. On our journey so much happens that upsets us, we are prone to turn around and go back to Babylon. These are the dark nights of the soul.

I most appreciate the Catholic writers on this subject. They seem to grant that these dark nights are critical to our spiritual development and we can't grow without them. It's hard to admit that in a sense we must face temptation and be beaten by it to grow, but that's what I hear them saying.

Solomon tells us that a primary characteristic of the righteous man is his ability to get back up after falling (Prov. 24:16), so falling into these dark nights is not a foreign experience for the righteous. Father Benedict Groeschel observes,

> Spiritual darkness is a psychological state of great discomfort, precipitated either by external causes like a painful loss or trauma or by inner conflicts leading to depression and a feeling of profound alienation. It can come from without like the death of a loved one or the failure of a cause; it may be from within, in which case it is really a breakdown of our defense pattern or a burnout, a kind of emotional and psychological exhaustion. It can be caused by sickness or imprisonment. It is important to take note of this because often people associate the spiritual darkness exclusively with spiritual aridity or some inner state. This misapprehension is probably caused by the fact that most books on the subject

are written by people who have nothing else to lose but their spiritual consolations. Hence the image of the cloistered nun kneeling on the flagstone floor in the frozen cloister is the popular image of the Dark Night. But I think most dark nights are experienced at kitchen tables and at office desks.[9]

I would add that these dark nights usually take place in the light of day. Other people never know that we are where we are. They think we are still functioning, believing, and acting responsibly, but inwardly we are dying, facing numerous demons seeking to destroy us. Our tendency is to deny the reality of what's happening, try to keep it a secret, and handle it within ourselves. But when we are stuck in a ditch and can't get out, the only thing to do is to stay put and hope that help comes from someplace. The time while we are stuck gives us serious "think time." It's a time when Soren Kierkegaard says we can really hear God's voice:

> Affliction is able to drown out every earthly voice, that is precisely what it has to do, but the voice of eternity within a man it cannot drown. Or conversely: it is the voice of eternity within which demands to be heard, and to make a hearing for itself it makes use of the loud voice of affliction. Then when by the aid of affliction all irrelevant voices are brought to silence, it can be heard, this voice within.[10]

Even in our temptations and afflictions the voice of God speaks to us. This is an excellent time to hear what He is saying.

Trials can produce extreme temptations, but even in the temptations we can hear the voice of God, wooing us back to Him, showing us who we really are and what we have to deal with in our lives. It's hard to deal with things alone, though.

A Teammate

The image of the solitary male of the American frontier dies hard. I'm not sure whether it was ever really true, but another frontier story provides an interesting contrast. Having spent one summer in Australia and a certain amount of time in the great Australian outback, I was fascinated by the difference between American and Australian males. On the Australian frontier, life was so difficult and the weather so severe that one could not survive without his mate. This mateship is regularly depicted in Australian movies *(The Man from Snowy River, A Town Like Alice, Gallipoli)*, which exalt the values of commitment to each other, even above women and society. To survive, one had to have a mate.

On a journey one needs a mate, but we as American men have not discovered the value of having fellow travelers in our lives. As noted in chapter 3, we romanticize about friends but do very little to cultivate male-male relationships.

The importance of having a teammate on the journey is paramount, especially during those dark nights when a man thinks no one else in the world understands him. He needs another man in his life who experiences his trials. This element is common in the Scriptures; yet, it is not regularly taught.

At the beginning of His ministry Jesus prayed all night and then called twelve men just to be with Him (Mark 3:14). His discipleship of them was largely sharing their life together as a group of men and enlisting others to that fraternity (1 John 1:1–3).

The apostle Paul is sometimes perceived to be a rugged, individualistic missionary, taking all the fiery shots of the enemy but continuing alone. Nothing could be further from the truth. Even though many credible writers call the "us's" and "we's" in his letters exhortatory plurals, the simplest explanation is that he was not alone when he wrote the letters and he alluded to the persons accompanying him on his journeys (Acts 20:4). The only recorded instance of his being alone was his waiting in Athens for his friends Silas and Timothy (Acts 17:16). At the end of his life when he was imprisoned, he was concerned because he was down to only one traveling companion. Only Luke was with him . . . in jail. But he asked for both Timothy and Mark to come to him (2 Tim. 4:11, 21).

Paul was not the individualist he is sometimes touted to be. He had teammates for his journey of life and his missionary endeavors. At times Paul says he despaired for his life. Those were dark nights, and God's comfort came to him in the comfort of a friend (2 Cor. 1:3–4; 7:5–7; 11:24–33).

> *Paul is not the individualist he is sometimes touted to be. He had teammates for his journey of life and his missionary endeavors.*

Spiritual development does not have an individual track; it is communal and relational. Men who do not have friends accompanying them on their journey may not be able to genuinely grow spiritually. I seriously doubt whether it is possible to grow spiritually with only a private faith. It is certainly difficult to apply all the "one anothers" in the Scripture when one is alone. We may prefer to travel alone, but when we're stuck in the mud, we need a friend to help us get out.

The Total Trip

The spiritual life is never finished in this life. We look for a city that is to come. However, we can look back and see where we have come from. When I look back, I see the total providential reality that God has literally used everything during the trip to develop me in some way. Even the times in the ditch, the wrong turns, and the blowouts are parts of the developmental trip. This helps me to better accept what may be coming around the next turn. I may fight it or not like it, but ultimately I know that it is part of my developmental journey.

A final vision John records in his Apocalypse is our looking back on our journey. When we see it, we see it in new ways. We see it as an expression of our Lord's creative design; nothing happened that did not in some way exist because He desired it (Rev. 4:11). This truth makes my manhood a little easier.

CHAPTER 10

Uneasy Conclusion
Or What Real Manhood
Is All About

———■———

Across America men are beginning to talk more openly about their unique approaches to life and their problems and how they relate to work, marriage, parenting, and everything else that demands their time and energy. A movement is emerging. Men are meeting together in small groups, for weekends, and one-on-one. This movement does not appear to be politically driven as was the women's movement over a decade ago. If anything, it is more personal than political, more spiritual than vocational. Men seem to be expressing the fact that all has not been well with them. Rather than accepting the definitions and interpretations of the male experience from the feminine movement, however, they are beginning to articulate their feelings in their own words and at their own pace.

Robert Bly's Gatherings of Men has become famous for getting men together to share a weekend or evening trying to better understand this thing called manhood. Bly confesses, "There is a lot of pain around men today, but this pain is more the unacknowledged grief they carry. Our heroes last until we are thirty-two or thirty-five, and then we begin to grieve for something that is missing within our souls." Bill Moyers explains these gatherings, "Men are drawn to gatherings like this one by a sense of loss, a loss of familiar myths and road maps, but also by a sense of hope. There is something optimistic about the very willingness of men to learn from one another through sharing the confusion over the problems of life."[1]

What I have tried to do in this book is to articulate where much of the confusion has been and to give a vision for hope. In this sense, it is one man's sharing his personal experience and frustration along with the experiences of many other men. Together, these experiences may provide a guide and create a desire for readers to take the same journey and to use the book as a beginning point for discussion and self-examination. Until men begin to share their confusion and their binds, hope for self-understanding is impossible. The confusion and grief we share seems to stem from a deep-seated loss we feel in our own manhood. If Bly is correct that "grief is the door to male feelings," then perhaps the preceding pages have cracked the door to some of the tensions and difficulties we men uniquely face—and then grieve over—the rest of our lives.

Until men begin to share their confusion and their binds, hope for self-understanding is impossible.

As I close, I will not try to fix anything or offer solutions that sound good but rarely work. I will try merely to better illumine the direction men might take to better understand how their inner life fits into a life with God and to perhaps gain a glimpse of what manhood is all about.

Goals of the Book

Throughout the book, I have tried to identify the difficulties and tensions that men face within themselves. In this sense, the book guides men on their quest for self-understanding and helps women better understand men. My hope is that a male reader will realize he is normal in what he feels and experiences; his experience as a man is a shared experience, common to this thing called maleness.

A second goal is to argue for a new kind of male—not the one so publicized as needed by the feminist movement, but one we might call a uniquely integrated male, one who experiences the full range of his manhood as a unity. I reflect again on my son and the memory of my childhood. It seems young boys are very integrated within themselves. They are spontaneous, expressive, aggressive yet fun-loving, and not too serious.

Something happens to them, however. They learn to conform, to color inside the lines, to stay clean, to be quiet, to dress up in coats and ties, and to look like the good little boys their mothers always wanted. They learn to departmentalize, rationalize, compromise, socialize, and standardize.

Our culture, schools, churches, and parents call it maturity. But I sometimes wonder if it really is or if something very special has been lost, especially when women want many of these qualities back in men. I also wonder why men feel so guilty or unnatural when they act a bit foolishly or break outside the traditional guidelines set forth by all the nurturing institutions. Much of the male mid-life crisis is about breaking out of these impossible bonds, which have only reduced the male to an institutionalized, functioning machine.

It's no surprise to me that men are not doing well. In every health statistic they do poorly compared to women. The price tag for being masculine is high in our culture. Leanne Payne has called attention to this masculine crisis: "Much called emotional illness or instability today is merely the unaffirmed masculine out of balance within the personality." She adds, "Very few men indeed are adequately affirmed as men today and many are pathologically split off from their masculine side altogether."[2]

The Fractured Male

What has brought about this fractured male? The integrated male who has both sides of his brain working and both sides of his personhood intact is indeed rare. The older, time-honored male with all his strength certainly had praiseworthy elements. He was heroic, virile, aggressive, and mostly externally engaging. But he was out of touch with the softer elements of his person that made for caring, sensitivity, and nurturing.

The newer male, created and carved out by the sexual revolution of the sixties, is a refreshing improvement for many women. However, even though he may be more in touch with his feelings and will share them, is a better nurturer at home, and is a better negotiator and compromiser in his relationships, his lack of many of the older leadership qualities is becoming increasingly apparent. Has this new male sacrificed being ambitious, seeking career goals, making a stand for important beliefs, and accepting challenges and conflicts for becoming what appears to be a weaker and wimpier kind of man?

Some women say they wish their husbands would be stronger, stand up to them, take charge, make decisions, and be more ambitious. I often wonder where they were in the sixties when we needed them! In a lead story of *USA Today*, the writer notes,

> Do women know what to do with this sensitive man when he arrives? As men search to balance machismo and sensitivity, both women and men seem confused by just how

touchy-feely the 90s man should be. . . . Today's woman is telling her man to open up. And when he does, she does not know how to react, when the sensitive male shows his insecurities, his fears, she does not like what she sees. Sometimes she will call him a wimp, the word has become a caricature to describe the indecisive, ambivalent male, the man who walks on egg shells, and really is afraid to say how he feels. Really what women *now* want is both qualities of strength and sensitivity.[3]

Isn't this great? Now the ladies have changed their minds! They now want both because they have decided that they don't like the purely sensitive male. This bind is even greater and makes our manhood next to impossible.

What Is Manhood?

So what is this thing called manhood? At this point, I want to discuss how I visualize the masculine experience and how we can become more integrated males. Talking about manhood is not fashionable today. In some circles I can't even use the word *manhood* because of its masculine overtones. We must speak in genderless terms. After I spoke to a group of men and women, a very sincere, well-meaning woman told me she was offended by my language. I knew I hadn't used profanity, so I had to ask what she meant. My use of *man* offended her; it was a dirty word to her. However, since this book is about men and for men, I *will* speak of what I believe *manhood* is all about.

Essence of Personhood

One cannot speak of male issues without addressing the bigger and broader question of personhood. I have a blatant bias here. I believe the essence of personhood lies in seeing ourselves as creational beings. To say this is to draw upon the long-standing tradition of generic man as the unique creation of

God. The biblical terminology is "the image of God." God made man in two kinds, male and female, and both were created in "the image of God." As a creational being, I am not an animal or a higher animal form. I am unique; I have significant present and eternal worth.

I am often amazed by how many leading social and psychological scientists argue for the intrinsic value of all human beings. Much of the current improving-your-self-image teaching has its basis in granting universal self-worth to every individual. But I have to ask, How do I really know I have value? Do I have value because a psychologist says I do or because a motivational speaker says I do? If I am the mere product of some evolutional chance, how do I derive human uniqueness and worth from this time plus chance equation? If anything, I am no more than the other animals who also got lucky and drew the winning ticket to survival!

Once you accept being made in the image of God and therefore having unique creatureliness, there is a lot more to the package. Being creational means having creational aspects, those aspects true about us as humans for which we have no explanation except that God made them. To argue that God made man in two kinds, male and female, is not so explosive since maleness and femaleness are rather obvious from the anatomical point of view. However, to argue for more than physical differences is often to place oneself in a precarious position and to be guilty of biology-equals-destiny logic. Although I don't believe in the biology-equals-destiny logic often attacked by certain feminists, I believe that biology equals and means something. Differences do exist, and they mean something. To ignore them is to ignore one of the most fundamental things about existence. One researcher suggests,

> Some of the intolerance about men that women talk about is directly related to this slanted perception of how things should be. Both genders have a natural "framework" which is healthy for them, but it may be damaging for the

opposite sex. . . . It's possible that this is just the way some men are, and women take it personally as if men are deliberately acting that way.[4]

One who argues for perceiving man as a creational being considers the male and the female made for each other. The view presupposes that maleness and femaleness are different and not to be confused. The words used in the Hebrew text for maleness and femaleness have Arabic roots, which mean "protruded one" and "perforated one," respectively.[5] The biblical understanding of sexuality roots itself firmly in anatomy, not psychology or sociology. If a person has a "protrusion," he is viewed as male; someone with a "perforation" is female. This seems fairly basic and fundamental, but it is no longer that simple. Many today argue that one is male if he feels malish (psychological understanding) or if he does the things a male should do in his culture (sociological interpretation).

Looking at his own physical anatomy, a man must at some point recognize that he was made to fit the other sex.[6] The creational conclusion is that humans are created for relationships.

The relationship is threefold as I see it. A person is made for the opposite sex, for God, and for an integrated life within oneself. The relational aspect in regard to the opposite sex is self-evident. The aspect of the relationship with God is not so evident. It is probably best evidenced in unfulfilled longings and the inabilities of other humans to fulfill a person totally. Many spouses are disillusioned by marriage because the partner could not meet every need. These persons begin with wrong assumptions about marriage and the nature of human fulfillment.

I believe no human being can fulfill another person in every way. Yet, something cries out within us that there must be more, there must be a fulfilling relationship somewhere. So we keep looking. These are our creational yearnings, longing for the One who created us. Saint Augustine put it simply, "There is a God-shaped vacuum in the heart of every man, and our hearts are restless until they find their rest in Thee."

Simplicity Fractured

A creational understanding of personhood also argues that man is a complex and a simple being at the same time; some are more simple and some are more complex than others. The complexity is evident in the physical, intellectual, emotional, moral, spiritual, and volitional aspects of man identified by various studies. Whole psychologies have been built on understanding each dimension and how it relates to the others. However, researchers also recognize that many pathological disturbances of the individual occur when these aspects are out of balance, that is, when the simplicity with which the individual desires to have all the elements of himself working together is out of whack.

The absentminded professor is laughable to everyone except his wife. He may be brilliant in his field (intellectual development), but his relational skills may be terrible. Ask him how he feels, and more often than not he will feel very uncomfortable but can't express it. He is an intellectualizer, not a feeler. He is brain dominant and out of balance within himself.

Take J. Edward Wall Street III. He is your standard type A, MBA-educated, goal-oriented, aggressive and willful man. He knows where he wants to go and how he is going to get there. Don't get in his way or you will have a conflict on your hands. He is volitionally dominant. But as is common today on Wall Street, the moral side of his personality has not grown in proportion to his will. Consequently, ethics and serious moral considerations are not vital to him. In fact, they get in the way of where he's going. His argument is, if it's not illegal, it must be moral!

Then there's Fred Fundamentalist. Every decision for him is a moral issue. Emotions or feelings of others have no place in his thinking. The only factor he considers is what the Bible says or what his religious group "says" the Bible says. Fred is also out of touch with himself. He is a policeman determined to enforce and abide by one big Law. He needs to learn to experience the feeling side of life in both himself and others.

For Art N. Craft, life is just as narrow. He is in touch with his feelings. In fact, he doesn't work if he doesn't feel like it; after all, his work is so feeling oriented. If he feels bad, there's no reason to work. For him, the sociopolitical or geopolitical ramifications of his trade are irrelevant. Even finances seem trivial. Moral considerations are laughable because if something feels good, it must be right! He is also out of balance and out of touch with much that is uniquely human and masculine.[7]

These short portraits grossly oversimplify human personalities, but they illustrate the point that men today are out of touch with much of what constitutes the creational aspects of personhood.

What Caused the Fracture?

Now the key question to raise is this: How do we account for this disruption and destruction of personhood? Why is finding a person with all the creational aspects in simple unity so difficult? Something has obviously happened. If God has made us to be unified beings experiencing the full range of our capabilities, why do we so struggle to find this unity within ourselves?

I remember taking a world religions class. One assignment was to determine the similarities and the critical differences of the world religions. A consistent commonality was that at some point in their early histories, God had created everything, and everything was good and perfect, but then something happened that made man and the entire creation less than perfect. In details there were many differences, but in overarching concepts the common assumption of human history was that man as he is now was not the way God (or the gods) made him. Something happened that brought about man's lowered state.

In the Bible, we know this concept to be the original sin of our first parents through which we inherit a nature that is not what God originally designed. Chuck Colson has said on numerous occasions, "There is more empirical evidence for the sinfulness of man than any other doctrine of human history. If so, I wonder why we so struggle to see it in ourselves?"

If this doctrine is difficult for you to accept, at least embrace it by faith on the basis of several millennia of written human history. Sin in the human personality means there is a creational contradiction within us. A fallen aspect woven into the fabric of our personalities affects who we are and everything we do. It affects our relationships, our work, our sexuality, our longings, and our motivations. It makes us more complex than God designed and accounts for our longing for simplicity and integration.

The contradiction hits me at many levels. I want to love, but I can't. I want to change, but I can't. I want to be more involved, but I don't. I want to get more organized, but I never do anything about it. I want to get out of things, but I stay in them. I want to build my relationships, but I tear them apart. I want to be successful, but I sabotage my efforts. O wretched man that I am, who will deliver me from this creaturely contradiction? Or putting the question in more developmental terms: If integration is possible, where and how does it begin?

The answer is as simple and complex as the question. If we are creatures caught in a fundamental contradiction of the personality, only an invasion and an infusion from without can be the remedy. That is easy to say—and it is the classic theme of historic Christianity—but bringing about change in the human personality through that invasion and infusion is not as easy as often touted. Many persons think that merely being born again suddenly and magically transforms the individual into something he wasn't before. The real good news is that integration *begins* with the invasion of the person of Jesus Christ into our consciousness and with the resultant infusion of a friendly Spirit (Holy One) into our personalities. This alien but friendly Spirit becomes the significant change agent in our personalities, bringing about new growth and creating new possibilities for integration.

Failure of Self-Helps

A remarkable assumption of the self-help movement centers on the human ability to bring about change within oneself. It seems very few are interested in questioning this basic axiom. Look at the self-help section in any bookstore. The entire gamut of human experiences and problems is found there neatly packaged in terms of some ten- or twelve-step program to bring about change in the human character. And those books sell! By the number of copies sold every year, one could safely conclude that we should be the most self-helped people in the world. But do they actually bring about change?

Researchers have been slow to investigate this area to see if the programs, books, and videos do what they claim to do. One psychologist at least wanted to evaluate his own field to determine if all the counseling was accomplishing anything and if a true psychological change was taking place within the individual. The title of his book reveals his conclusions: *The Shrinking of America: Myths of Psychological Change.* He says,

> Our culture is strongly committed to the proposition that people are highly malleable. Three key assumptions of the present age are that human beings should change because they are not as competent or as good or as happy as they could be; that there are few limits to the alterations they can make; and that change is relatively easy to effect. If only the right methods are used and the right attitudes are held, people can make significant changes and become almost whatever they want.[8]

In his conclusion he suggests another approach:

> I cannot say for certain that we will be happier if we let go of some of our fantasies and some of our preoccupation

with altering ourselves, but there are benefits. Acceptance of ourselves as we are, and this would include acceptance of our desire to be different than we are, would mean less disappointment and less self-hatred for not being all the things we believe we should be. A fair amount of money now spent on attempts at modifying ourselves would be saved, money that might be better spent on other comforts, and amusements. Acceptance can provide a clearer picture of reality, no longer seen through the spectacles of utopian possibilities and I think this clearer view would be refreshing. If we stop trying to change everything about ourselves and others, we may develop a better understanding of what can be readily changed and do better jobs of dealing with those things, and also of what can't be changed and so stop trying to do the impossible.[9]

The book was not a best-seller, but his documentation was as thorough as it was disturbing.

> *The failure of self-help programs is that they both begin and end with the Self.*

The failure of self-help programs is that they both begin and end with the Self. It is very difficult for the Self to change itSelf because the Self will always bring about changes that reflect what the Self really is . . . its own Self. Self always makes changes made in its own image. Therefore, the only true change is the change brought about by an outside source with an outside orientation point. It must be extraneous to the human Self.

Integration Begins

Christ: The Integration Point

Jesus Christ is able to achieve this change in His followers. He invites us, "Come to Me, all you who labor and are heavy laden, and I will give you rest. . . . And you will find rest for your souls" (Matt. 11:28–29). Jesus then becomes the new orientation point for our lives. His acceptance and forgiveness become the keys to making a new start wherever we are in our lives. He has invited us to come, and He will never reject us, for He has said, "My sheep hear My voice, and I know them, and they follow Me. And I give them eternal life, and they shall never perish; neither shall anyone snatch them out of My hand" (John 10:27–28).

Just as we are created to be oriented to God Himself but have become disoriented through sin, now through being followers of Christ, we begin the reorientation and reorganization of our lives around God. Many people talk about "focus" today. They say, "I need to find focus, or I just can't focus like I should." They are admitting in their fallen humanity that they have lost their orientation point, but still being in the image of God, they have a residual longing for "focus." That's found only in Christ.

A Friendly Spirit: The Source of Integration

Having an integration point by itself doesn't bring about change. For the change to bring about integration, it must take place in the deep recesses of the human spirit. That is why Christ said to His followers, "It is to your advantage that I go away; for if I do not go away, the Helper [Holy Spirit; John 14:26] will not come to you; but if I depart, I will send Him to you" (John 16:7). The Holy Spirit in some mysterious and mystical way indwells our consciousness, combines with our own spirits (personalities), and infuses us with divine life and capabilities.[10]

The Spirit begins the process of reintegration within the individual, bringing him or her back into the creational unity that was lost through sin. In this life, the process is never complete because of our fallen natures, but the reintegration process brings about significant changes. Although I don't believe there are fundamental changes within the human personality

——217——

(an extrovert doesn't become an introvert, etc.), there will be a new awareness of areas of the self. Men might have new feelings of either strength or caring, whichever was underdeveloped in their pre-Christ days. At the same time, they have a new dynamic for development. In essence, the Holy Spirit provides for the follower of Christ both a restraining influence and a restorative dynamic.

Having been with Christ for almost twenty-five years now, I am amazed by two things. First, I am not as bad as I could be. When I think about my life and the things that tempt me and the things that I give in to, something inside me restrains much of what I do. Some might write it off as socialization or good parenting or the fear of consequences, but I know it is more than that. There is a presence within and without that I cannot explain, that works through my mind and will to keep me from being as evil and ugly as I could be.

The other phenomenon unexplainable to me is the staying power of this presence within me. Even though I do not always act in accordance with what I know is right, that haunting presence continues to convict me, encourage me, and keep me from giving up. I know this is far more than mere human steadfastness. I am constantly and silently aware that I am more than just a son to my human father; I am also a child of God. Though I fail, God is still my Father, and I am still His child. We are told very clearly that this is the work of an alien Spirit within, telling us that "we are children of God" (Rom. 8:16).

Before I try to define what Christian manhood is all about or at least what truly Christian manhood might look like, I must reveal my difficulty with many books on the subject. There are many very helpful books on men's issues today, but they fall into two camps. One group takes a developmental approach and uses the available research on men's issues to argue for a distinctive male psychology. These are usually strong on the psychological and developmental aspects but silent or weak on spiritual integration. The other group relies heavily on Scripture and an understanding of men from a spiritual point of view. However, these are limited to biblical passages and biblical metaphors. One current best-seller takes a problem-solution approach; the male reader locates the problem he faces and then refers to a list of passages to read with some suggested helps. I know many men who have been helped by this approach, but it's too canned for me. Life is not that simple and it ignores the whole field of adult male development. In this last chapter I am attempting to argue for an approach to manhood that is both distinctively developmental and spiritually grounded.

Christian Manhood

So what does Christian manhood look like? First, it is manhood that is characteristically masculine or manly. Every aspect of a man's being will be experienced distinctively, and in some way the Spirit of God connects with this uniqueness. If the sexual distinctions mean anything at all, they mean that something is dominant and something else is secondary. Though there are always exceptions, we know that men generally are more left-brain dominant than right-brain. Therefore, their thinking abilities are more aligned with logic, rational processes, and abstraction. They are likely to be abstract about very emotional, feeling-related issues. Herb Goldberg alludes to this ability:

> The male . . . is comfortable with ideas and abstractions, not emotions. He relates in staccato fashion, with no "flow." He is the opposite of the femininely defensive woman who can talk for long stretches of time about her feelings and can probe her experience incessantly but is bored by discussions about mechanical problems or abstract issues.[11]

He also points out that this difference in intellectualizing process becomes the ground for perceiving the whole arena of relationships:

[The male] avoids any spontaneous personal involvement that doesn't have a goal or purpose or doesn't approach him slowly. He experiences it as a pressure, as loss of control, a demand to be involved. If he withdraws to regain his balance, she perceives this as a rejection. So he feels pressured to have to reassure her constantly that he's not rejecting her.[12]

As noted earlier, Carol Gilligan's work at Harvard indicated men view relationships of closeness as threatening while women view separateness as violence. These fundamental differences don't go away just because one is a follower of Christ.

Even in moral dilemmas, men and women approach ethical issues differently. In Kohlberg's classic studies of moral development, he retold the often-used moral dilemma of Joseph Fletcher. Fletcher related the story of a Jewish woman in a Russian camp during World War II; she was married, with a family on the outside. The dilemma is created by a Russian guard who says that if she gets pregnant, she will be allowed to go home, and he volunteers to get her pregnant.

Kohlberg found that men approached the dilemma abstractly, almost coldly. If they valued the family more highly than they disapproved infidelity, the solution was argued that it was acceptable for her to get pregnant. On the other hand, if they believed infidelity was a serious breach of the moral covenant of marriage, it didn't matter that her family needed her or she needed them. On both counts, they argued purely on the basis of principle.

Women inevitably asked for more information to get the relational component. Their approach was more situational. They would ask, "How long have they been married? How old are the kids? Are they in love? How long has she been in prison? How good looking is the guard?"[13] The whole process was fairly cut-and-dried for men, but women needed more information before they could make a decision.

Another area of difference commonly observed but rarely

admitted is that of humor. To prove this point, when I speak to groups made up of both men and women, I tell a joke and then note who laughs and who is offended. Here is the joke. Two men who were good friends were playing golf. Across from their hole, a funeral procession passed. One man took off his cap and placed it reverently over his heart. His friend was quite taken by this honoring of the procession. He said, "I didn't know you felt so deeply about such things." "Well," his friend answered, "this one's a little special. That's my wife in the hearse!" Men, especially the golfers, usually laugh. But women exclaim, "That's terrible!" There's a fundamental difference somewhere.

To equalize this humor point, I'll include a true story told on "The Tonight Show Starring Johnny Carson." A woman was fortunate to obtain one of the sold-out tickets to the Broadway musical "Phantom of the Opera." When she sat down, she noticed the seat on her left was empty. Just before showtime, she leaned over and spoke to the woman on the other side. She admitted her surprise at seeing a vacant seat since tickets were so rare. The other woman replied, "Well, the seat was to be my husband's, but he died recently." The woman answered, "Oh, that's terrible. Couldn't you have gotten someone to use the ticket?" "No," she blurted, "I didn't have time. The funeral is going on right now!" Women laugh at this one, but men somehow don't think it's funny. Touché.

The purpose of highlighting these differences is not to suggest that one sex is more right than the other but to illustrate that men and women think differently in every area.[14] This also affects the way they approach the Christian life. When we add to these differences the better-known hormonal, sexual, and physical differences, it should be more than evident that what is needed is not only a distinctively masculine psychology but also a distinctively masculine spirituality. With the feminization of our society I fear that even our assumptions about the Christian life are regarded as something more for women than for men. I contend that the spiritual life experienced by males will differ widely from that experienced by females.

What enthuses me spiritually may not enthuse my wife, and the other way around. Just as in every area of life, when I engage my personhood to the spiritual realm, I will do it with my distinctive male approaches. I will pray as a man, care as a man, give as a man, involve myself as a man, and react and respond as a man. I don't leave my maleness at the church door. The wise church would realize this obvious fact and ask what it can do to more uniquely tailor itself to men.

Christly Manhood

The second part to answering my question about manhood is recognizing that Christian manhood will also be distinctively Christly. Yes, Christly; that is, uniquely like Christ. There is certainly no lack of material on what Christlikeness involves. However, my experience with this material is that it somehow always ends up saying, "Be good." Knowing that I will always fail to meet the impossible standards of Christlikeness does not encourage me about the Christian life.

Most of us men adopt a tolerable relationship with the Christian standards with minimal expectations for fulfillment and call it Christianity. If anything, the Christian life is reduced to merely trying to do the best we can in any situation. But often this breeds more failure and shame and reinforces the cycle of unacceptability that seems to accompany so much of our spiritual experience. We need a different model, a true model. The only model I know that balances true humanity with divine life is the life of Christ.

To understand what the Christian life is really like, men need to look at the life of Christ. In His life, we will see a truly masculine life lived out with spiritual commitments. In Jesus, they were never in contradiction, never departmentalized, never out of balance. In Him, we can see the full range of the masculine experience driven by divine life. I believe this fully integrated life is what the Spirit of God is trying to produce in men today. It is not a churchy, phony, unrealistic life. It is an engaging life, filled with human emotion, feeling, and tension, yet never without divine perspective, meaning, and purpose. It is the kind of life I believe men are looking for in many other places.

Jesus' life was perfectly integrated. But it was not perfect in the way we usually think of perfection. You may discover some surprises as you read. The portrait of His life shows us what God would like to see in our lives.

Integration of Strength and Compassion

Much is known of the compassion of Christ. However, sometimes His strengths are overshadowed by the common "weak and pale" picture. The older I get, the more I value men who can stand for the truth and their beliefs. Jesus did, even to the point of driving out the merchants in the Jewish temple (Matt. 21:1–13). This would be comparable to walking into the New York Stock Exchange and pulling the computer plugs, throwing the whole place into turmoil.

On many occasions Jesus went against the cultural norms and refused to submit to the traditions of men, which were meaningless or presented a false view of spirituality (Luke 11:37–41). He didn't play games with people's lives and faith. He took extreme risks everywhere He went, and He also defended His followers from attacks (Matt. 15:1–14). Apparently, He didn't let opposition get to Him, and He prepared His followers for it (Matt. 10:16–23). One time He called a group of religious leaders "whitewashed tombs . . . full of dead men's bones" (Matt. 23:27). In that culture, with that group of people, His words were probably equivalent to profanity. He was profaning what was considered sacred! With the same group of people Jesus didn't pull any punches. He told them what He thought of them (what they were) and pronounced a severe series of "woes" upon them.

When we look at Jesus this way, it's no wonder He got cruci-fied. He appeared to many powerful people as a cultural an-tagonist, a religious reactionary, and at times a political revolutionary. He certainly didn't resemble many males today, just trying to play the game to survive while compromising many masculine strengths in the process. But Jesus was not all strength.

His compassion was evident. He wept over a dead friend (John 11:35); He had mercy on lepers (Luke 17:12–14); He approached and healed "unclean" women (Mark 5:25; 7:26); His heart felt compassion toward a rich yuppie who wouldn't give up his material toys (Mark 10:21). When He looked on the multitudes, all He could see was their lack of leadership, and He felt compassion for them (Mark 8:2). The list could go on.

It would be hard to open any passage of the Gospels and not find some element of His compassion. The same is true for His strength. The conclusion? The two qualities were not contra-dictory or out of balance. They were perfectly integrated in one Person, a Man. I believe our alien but friendly Spirit seeks to develop these same qualities in us.

Some men may need more strength, others more compas-sion. In a strange way, compassion doesn't make any sense without strength or strength without compassion. Until we are capable of both, the one we have loses its value. A man who is compassionate all the time may be a wimp; he needs strength. A man who is strong all the time may be a tyrant or an angry young or old man.

Integration of Intellect and Emotion

Joe Tanenbaum indicates that men relate to the world and their immediate environment with either their heads or their bodies.[15] If they can't figure something out (intellect), they re-act physically (body). However, the feeling side (emotion) is kept safely hidden. Men do not do their investigative work at the feeling level. That is the domain of women. Tanenbaum records that his studies of homosexual men confirm his assumptions about the head and the body. Homosexual men pride themselves on being more feeling oriented and capable of understanding women better than most men, but Tanenbaum says they don't do any better than heterosexual men.[16]

What do we find in the life of Christ? We find a man who masterfully engaged His environment at the intellectual-level. When He was twelve years old, His dialogue with the rabbis sent shock waves around the temple compound (Luke 2:46–47). His arguments and logic silenced even the most brilliant of His day (Matt. 22:46). He even seems to have successfully tongue-tied the Roman procurator, Pontius Pilate (John 18:36). We can only smile at His intellectual abilities in creating ingenious intellectual dilemmas for His adversaries (Matt. 22:41–45).

Even His use of Scripture was novel. The only time we see anything that appears like a "Bible study" was after His resurrection when He proved who He was from the Scriptures (Luke 24:27). All other references to His use of Scripture were in the context of life, as allusions or as questions, asking others what a passage meant to them (Matt. 9:13; 21:42; 22:42–44). He knew the Scripture but skillfully and sensitively called on it to reveal where others were in their journey. In each instance, however, we see the heart of a feeler as well as the head of a thinker.

Jesus loved men (Mark 10:21; John 13:23). Some members of the gay community have tried to make Jesus into one of them because of His special relationship with men. In reality their effort highlights how unthinkable it is in our culture for a man to genuinely love another man in nonsexual ways. Jesus enjoyed the company of men and asked for their love of Him and one another (John 13:34; 21:15–17).

Jesus also experienced many other human emotions. He got tired (Mark 6:31). He was angered and grieved at the same time (Mark 3:5). He was astounded by and marveled at faith coming from one who shouldn't have had it (Matt. 8:10). As

He looked at Jerusalem for the last time before His death, He issued an emotional lament over His beloved nation (Matt. 23:37–39). He experienced agony and anxiety (Luke 22:44) and temptation (Matt. 4:1). He entered into the social joys of community life and ceremonies (Matt. 9:10; John 2:1) and told wonderful stories and one-liners reflecting a great sense of humor (Matt. 19:24).

In Jesus, the intellectual abilities work in perfect unison with the emotions. He moves from one to the other without contradiction. They were not in conflict as they are in so many men today. He was not unmasculine to weep or be tired or be angry or be anxious or enjoy a party. He was not being an intellectual to engage in serious dialogue about serious issues.

Many men today think that one is not really a man unless he is a businessman (who is often interpreted to be a pragmatic nonthinker). Men who think, and think seriously, about things need to be in towers someplace, preferably ivy-covered ones, they say. But there is a critical need for serious thinking in the streets . . . in business, in the church, in politics, and in foreign affairs. The survival of our way of life depends on it. We have to live in the present but also think about the future.

Integration of Present and Future

One thing I admire most about Jesus' capabilities is the way He approached people. He never asked them how they had gotten into the jams they were in. He didn't ask the woman caught in adultery, "Now, why are you committing this heinous crime with this man?" He didn't inquire into anyone's background (of course, being omniscient, He didn't need to). He met people in the present, right where they were in their lives. No matter what the situation, Jesus was a realist. He met all people—whether religious leaders, lepers, women, children, or His own disciples—where they were and dealt with them accordingly. However, He did not leave men where He found them.

He was also an idealist in the sense that He moved people into the future. He would not allow the woman caught in her sin to remain in her sin; He encouraged her to go and sin no more (John 8:11). He told the healed lepers to show themselves to the priests, and Zacchaeus, to make restitution (Luke 17:14; 19:1–10). After coming to grips with His countrymen's rejection of His messianic claims, He moved to the future and gave the hope of a future Jerusalem and national restoration (Matt. 23:39; 24:29). The present and the future were always integrated in Jesus, unlike the situation of many men today.

Some men live in the past exclusively. One man told me that his life has been going downhill since high school! These men are somehow alive in the present, but they long for the past and their short-lived glories as athletes, leaders, and Mr. Popular. Other men don't really want to think about the future. They are too busy fighting the alligators to seriously think about where their lives might be in ten years. They keep spending and borrowing to meet current needs. Some men live for the future, hoping and praying that it will be better. They sacrifice the present on the altar of the future, and their wives, kids, and relationships often suffer. Perhaps we can learn from Jesus that our relationship to time is our relationship to life— all of it, not just the present or the future.

Integration of All Aspects of Life

I have come to the conclusion that today's men need a non-religious faith. Men so hate religion or what it stands for that somehow we need to teach men that it is OK to be nonreligious and still be spiritual. The *Leadership* article on men quoted earlier also revealed that "Men want to fellowship with men without being 'churchy.' To many men, being churchy means being artificial, removed from the real world. They want none of it."[17] I believe that is precisely what I find in the life of Jesus, a nonreligious expression of spiritual manly life. Jesus didn't do any of the things He was supposed to do to be considered religious by His culture. Wherever it comes from, men have a deep-seated fear of being perceived as religious or overly religious.

> **Men have a deep-seated fear of being perceived as religious or overly religious.**

This fear becomes apparent when I have lunch with men in restaurants. As Christian men, we know that it is appropriate to say grace before we eat. But what about when business partners or nonbelievers are with us? One man said to me, "Shall we rub our eyebrows together?" In other words, let's make it look like, to each other, we are praying, but those around us won't know we are doing something weird like praying in a restaurant! A Jewish friend put a standing benediction on the restaurants we frequented, which was valid until they changed either the food or the prices. We could get down to eating faster and easier that way. By the way, I don't believe this is a scriptural absolute; there are many ways to express thanks without having to close one's eyes.

So what about Jesus and this nonreligious faith? Consider what He did. Jesus fished and cooked outdoors (John 21:12). He liked to eat, drink (real wine, I believe), and party (Mark 2:16). He attended weddings (John 2:2), funerals (John 11:17), and the Jewish Feasts of Passover and Tabernacles (Luke 22:15; John 7:2). He felt comfortable with many persons the religious community shunned: Samaritans (John 4:5–6), children (Matt. 19:13), a Roman centurion (Matt. 8:5), a Canaanite woman (Matt. 15:21–22), and an unclean woman with a difficult menstrual period (Mark 5:25).

When we think about our present age with the usual list of things that we men should do to be religious, I don't discover any of them in the life of Christ. He didn't attend Bible studies or prayer meetings; He didn't "go witnessing"; His attendance at "religious" meetings usually caused problems; and He certainly didn't go to meetings for the mere sake of being there. What He did was to be fully integrated into life. Yes, He prayed. Yes, He gave witness to God everywhere He went. Yes, He knew and used Scripture. Yes, He enjoyed the fellowship of like-minded believers. But all of those activities were genuinely integrated with life.

We men are so prone to departmentalizing our lives that the spiritual life gets boxed into the category of "church." Since we don't like church or religious things, our spiritual development suffers. We need to see that the life of the spirit can invade all of life. We can pray at work or in the car and not pray over lunch if it seems inappropriate. We can enjoy non-Christian things because Jesus did.

We don't have to be bound to traditional categories of viewing people; we can see people for who they are without reference to getting a sale or gaining personal benefit. We can enjoy our sports, our hobbies, and our families as true spiritual expressions of our faith. We choose to do what we do in the church not because we want to be more religious but because we genuinely care about what happens there. In the process, we show forth what an integrated life looks like, and this life ends up being a witness to the life of God in all our relationships.

Integration of Purpose and Freedom

As noted earlier, men seek to control their environment, and they are goal oriented and operate on the basis of purpose. Women can shop but never buy. A shopping expedition with nothing concrete to show for it would be purposeless to men. Why shop if you don't intend to buy anything? Consequently, men have problems going with the flow, adjusting to novelty or the unexpected. These characteristics get at the difficulty of integrating a sense of purpose and a sense of freedom. Again, let's examine the life of Jesus.

Jesus certainly had His vocational purpose established early in His career (Calvinists would say from eternity past). It is clear throughout the Gospels that He had a compulsion to carry out His Father's will in the world and to do His Father's work (John 17:4). He acknowledges He had accomplished this work. He was bothered when His disciples did not take the sense of mission seriously with all its implications (Matt. 16:23). He passionately set His face toward the work and its accomplishment (Luke 9:51) and passed the work on to His disciples (John 17:18). As a man, He knew where He needed to go and what needed to be accomplished. He allowed nothing, including the forces of evil, to stand in the way of the mission. Yet, as we read the Gospel accounts, we never feel He is in a hurry, compulsively deals with people, or forces people to do what He wants them to do.

On the contrary, He said at the outset that followership is voluntary, based on one's desire (Matt. 16:24), and He asked men only to come and check Him out and where He was going (John 1:39, 43). There was no arm-twisting or guilt motivation. He asked hurting people if they wanted to get well (John 5:6). He didn't force His agenda on others. He allowed His own people to reject Him, even when He could have used His divine abilities more to prove who He was. But He said they were "not willing" to accept Him on the basis of His claims (Matt. 23:37). He also added that He will not come back *until* they are willing (Matt. 23:39)! He doesn't force belief on anyone but grants the rights of sonship to those who receive Him (John 1:12).

> *To many goal-oriented men, letting people do what they want to do, not being in charge in the sense that outcomes must be predictable, measurable, and obtainable, would seem like weakness.*

To many goal-oriented men, letting people do what they want to do, not being in charge in the sense that outcomes must be predictable, measurable, and obtainable, would seem like weakness.

Jesus had His priorities, but He apparently wasn't MBO trained—Management by Objectives wasn't part of His agenda. If anything, He "managed" more by the other person's objectives.

On one occasion, He kept a very important synagogue official waiting, to whom He had made a prior commitment, in order to help a woman who had had the same problem for twelve years (Mark 5:21–43). His delay did more than aggravate the official; the delay cost the life of the official's daughter. Of course, Jesus healed her. But how many men would have broken the "planned" agenda to meet a spontaneous, nonurgent problem? That behavior doesn't fit the normal world of work today. But in Jesus, being purposeful and granting human freedom and being free in His life were not contradictions.

Probably the first conflict I experienced in my marriage was over this issue. I have a very spontaneous wife. When we took one of those personality inventories, I was off the chart on discipline, and she went the other way on flexibility. After over twenty years of marriage, I think I have learned to be more flexible and recognize that being flexible is not contrary to having goals and plans. I still have to plan the spontaneity, but at least it appears spontaneous to her. In Jesus, these qualities found a perfect integration. I hope God's Spirit will continue to bring about this integration in my life and make my marriage more easy.

Speaking of women, we also need to see how Jesus related to the opposite sex.

Integration of Strength and Sensitivity with Women

After the sixties, Jesus became a hero to feminists. They liked the way He related to women and exalted their status, often against the cultural male-dominated norms. He did those things, to the dismay and anger of some men today. However, some feminists didn't tell the whole story. Jesus exalted the status of women in the first century, even to the point of praising what was then a purely masculine role of sitting at the feet of a rabbi (Luke 10:38–42). He affirmed Mary's role over the traditional role of women in the kitchen where Martha, her sister, was. He also accepted financial support from a group of women (Luke 8:3), which raises all kinds of interesting issues in their culture and ours. He also defended the woman caught in adultery and brought to light the injustice of the whole process (John 8:10–11). His sensitivity to women is well known.

However, often overlooked are the times He seems somewhat blunt, if not rude, to women. He was very forceful with His mother when she was out of place in asking Him to do some things that were not part of His messianic plan (John 2:4; see also Matt. 12:46–50). We also forget that in affirming Mary's role, He was putting down Martha's compulsive concern about the kitchen.

How about when Jesus asked the woman at the well to call her husband? He knew she had five of them, and the one she was living with at the present time wasn't her own (John 4:16). That rather pointed statement went straight to the heart of her failures.

Jesus' reply to the Canaanite woman seems so insensitive. She had an urgent need to remove the demon from her daughter, but He said, "Let the children [of Israel, by implication] be filled first, for it is not good to take the children's bread and throw it to the little dogs" (Mark 7:27). Canaanites were commonly called dogs, not a very flattering term then or now. But Jesus called her a dog. She heard Him accurately and picked up on the metaphor: "Yet even the little dogs under the table eat from the children's crumbs." He then told her that her daughter was healed.

I remind you of these passages so that we don't conveniently leave certain passages out of the profile that don't fit our contemporary "enlightened" male perspective. This balanced profile tells me that within Jesus was an integration between strength and sensitivity with reference to women. I hate to make this next statement, but I feel I must. It seems Jesus had the sense to know when He needed to be sensitive to a woman and when He needed to be stronger with her and put her in her place. Ouch! Why is this so difficult for men today?

For one thing, serious employment issues are related to it. Try to be tough with women on the job today, and they can cry gender discrimination. Men are fired without explanation. I once asked a female psychologist, "Why is it so difficult for a group of men leaders in the church to effectively deal with problem women?" Without hesitating, she replied, "Because men aren't supposed to hit women!" I believe we have compromised something here. Just as some men need compassion and understanding and others need a kick in the pants, so some women need the same, whether they wear pants or not!

> *True masculinity and true spirituality mean having the ability to be both strong and sensitive with women without contradicting or compromising either.*

True masculinity and true spirituality mean having the ability to be both strong and sensitive with women without contradicting or compromising either. This same quality carries over into the other important relationship of our lives: dealing with parents.

Integration of Parental Honor and Independence

Every Sunday the president of a fairly large corporation was required to have dinner at his parents' home. The stresses of parental expectations on him as an adult male and on his wife and family increased with time. Finally, he asked me what I thought he should do. My frank reply focused on trying to show him that honoring does not mean obeying. A showdown was apparently coming, and I encouraged him not to lose it! He needed to assert his manhood for both himself and his family.

—— 233 ——

Apparently, Jesus did the same thing. Jesus obeyed His parents when He was a child, even at the age of twelve, the age of Jewish manhood (Luke 2:51). But when He was an adult, His relationship with His mother changed.[18] He had to make it very clear to her that His vocational calling was establishing a different relationship between the two of them (Matt. 12:46–50). He clarified for His followers that all human relationships must be placed under their allegiance to Him (Matt. 10:37). And even though Jesus met His mother's request at the wedding, he made it clear that was no longer His role as her Son (John 2:4). However, in keeping with the Jewish tradition of honoring mothers (Exod. 20:12), before He was crucified, Jesus made sure her care would be provided by one of His disciples (John 19:27).

Jesus models for us as men a difficult aspect of our manhood: that of breaking free from our parents. Jesus honored His parents but was also independent to pursue His calling. These were not in contradiction but in unity. Men should not feel guilty (or be made to feel guilty) for breaking free from parents. However, the responsibility of honoring is lifelong. Honoring means valuing and granting the respect due one's parents just because they were one's parents.

Conclusion of the Conclusion:
Where Have All the Mentors Gone?

What all these qualities illustrate in the life of Jesus is the unique combination of grace and truth incarnated in one Man (John 1:17). Truth is the strength factor, knowing what one believes and is willing to act on to demonstrate what is truly important. Men need truth in order to be the warriors in the marketplace, the defenders of important values in our society. To be manly means to live on the basis of truth, not only to have relations that speak the truth and deal honestly with people but also to live with such integrity within oneself that the real person is never compromised.

Grace is the quality that gives and gives in when the situation warrants it. This, however, is not a wimpy kind of give-in-ness. It is a self-giving rooted in truth and right action. When I sacrifice myself for the sake of higher values and principles, it is not weakness. It is a strength that chooses to give of oneself because of more important reasons. Granting favor when favor is not deserved is not weakness. Giving in is not "caving in" if love is the motive. God so loved the world He gave and sacrificed His own Son to meet man at the point of his greatest need. God did not compromise His character to do this. It was a pure expression of His gracious character. So it is with men.

Seeing these qualities in harmony within ourselves will never be realized perfectly in this life. To be such is an impossible task and even more so when we realize women say they want men who are both strong and sensitive. However, what usually reigns in my life is some confusion of the qualities or an unhealthy imbalance of the two. I wish I had both equally. But I am encouraged to know that both qualities existed harmoniously in my Lord, and if He is involved in my life, then He is still not finished with me. I'm still growing and developing, and as a pilgrim I'm not yet home. I'm still looking for the city that is to come. Knowing Him and knowing that He knows me makes my manhood considerably easier, although it will never be easy.

Yet as much as Jesus is the model of manhood I value most greatly, I still wonder where the modern men are who value the soulish values, who desire a mentoring experience with other men. Where are the men who have been mentored or have a vision for mentoring and nurturing younger men?

Robert Bly and other developmental researchers suggest that for a boy to become a man there must exist the active intervention of older men in the lives of younger men. More often than not, however, older men have betrayed the younger men by their silence or by their active competition with them, and the younger men are now distrustful. At the same time, younger men yearn for the interaction and life instruction that older men have to give. Without the benefit of each other's mutual contribution, the issues and mysteries of manhood remain a secret. The axiom of "men don't talk" is perpetuated, and men silently grieve the loss of significant male understanding

> *Younger men yearn for the interaction and life instruction that older men have to give.*

and acceptance. Older men tragically accept their unrecognized grief and just believe this is the way men are. They pretend life is fine and don't share their struggles and insights with younger men. As a result, young men grow up to perpetuate the myth and betray the very feelings they so wanted other men to understand.

Male readers, I ask you to examine where your hurts, pains, and struggles have been. If you are younger, look around for older men with whom you can be honest and who can validate your feelings. If you're older, identify the life experiences that have been most meaningful to you. Think through what your life message might be to younger men. Realize that even though you think younger men may think you have nothing to give, you have much that they need and long for. You have a life that has been entrusted to you and to you alone. If you don't share it with someone else, you have missed one of the greatest opportunities of life.

A younger generation of men is listening for and desperately needs your voice. Who else in this fatherless culture can affirm young men in their maleness and initiate them in the rites of the male experience? If you don't define what maleness is in this culture, then young men will continue to look to women to define and affirm maleness. When we allow women to define our identities, our feelings, and our boundaries, the result will be a sense of loss. This emotion is usually experienced as a quiet inner rage toward life and all its expectations. The fault is not theirs, it is ours. We have settled for a manhood made in the image of women and not men. We must get our own act together and be men among men first. Then, we can form authentic relationships and carry out our responsibilities without having so much of our fragile identity at stake. We will begin to grow as men no matter what our age. Without this understanding our manhood will remain uneasy.

Epilogue

———■———

A Mandate from Our Mentor

1. You don't have to be in control of everything and have it all together.
2. It's OK to cry once in a while.
3. You can be gentle and see many rewards.
4. You don't need all the toys, perks, and affairs to be happy. You can be satisfied in doing the right thing.
5. The way you treat others is the way they will treat you. Be kind.
6. You don't have to spread yourself so thin you never see God.
7. You don't have to win every argument, close every deal, or be successful to be a good son.
8. You can risk your job if you think you are right.
9. Don't worry about what people think or say about you if you are doing what is right.

10. You are not the only one who has been fired for doing what is right. Celebrate! You stand in a long line of real men!

—Author's paraphrase of Matthew 5:1–12

Notes

Introduction
1. Allis, "What Do Men Really Want?" p. 80.

Chapter 1
1. From *The Family, a Report to the President*, from the White House Working Group on the Family, pp. 13–14.
2. Quoted by Joy on the tape, "The Innate Differences Between Males and Females."
3. Blitchington, *Sex Roles and the Christian Family*, p. 109.
4. Restak, *The Brain*, pp. 230–31.
5. Family Research Council, *Changes in the American Family*, p. 1.
6. Family Research Council, *Changes in the American Family*, p. 5.
7. Osherson, *Finding Our Fathers*, p. 4.
8. Goldberg, *The Hazards of Being Male*, p. 5.

Chapter 2
1. Gerzon, *Choice of Heroes*, p. 5.
2. Gerzon, *Choice of Heroes*, p. 13.
3. Goldberg, *The Hazards of Being Male*, p. 5.
4. Allis, "What Do Men Really Want?" p. 82.
5. Allis, "What Do Men Really Want?" p. 81.
6. Gilligan, *In a Different Voice*, p. 22.
7. Gilligan, *In a Different Voice*, p. 42.

8. Restak, *The Brain*, pp. 226–28.
9. Wheeler, *Time* special edition, p. 80.
10. Allis, "What Do Men Really Want?" p. 81.
11. Dittes, *The Male Predicament*, p. xii.
12. One of the men takes the baby into a restaurant bathroom to change the diaper and holds the baby's posterior up to the fan-driven hand dryer!
13. Allis, "What Do Men Really Want?" p. 82.

Chapter 3
1. Naifeh and Smith, *Why Can't Men Open Up?*, p. 62.
2. Lewis and Sussman, *Men's Changing Roles in the Family*, p. 165.
3. Naifeh and Smith, *Why Can't Men Open Up?*, p. 60.
4. Quoted in *Why*, p. 61.
5. Lewis and Sussman, *Men's Changing Roles in the Family*, p. 164.
6. Quoted in *Why*, p. 66.
7. Quoted in *Why*, p. 66.
8. Smith, *The Friendless American Male*, pp. 13–22.
9. Scher, *Handbook of Counseling and Psychotherapy with Men*, p. 31.
10. Druck, *The Secrets That Men Keep*, pp. 109–10.
11. Levinson, *The Seasons of a Man's Life*, p. 335.

Chapter 4
1. Newman, *Falling from Grace*, p. 69.
2. Hendricks and Sherman, *Your Work Matters to God*, p. 17.
3. Wingren, *Luther on Vocation*, p. 9.
4. Wagner, *The New Pilgrims*, p. 140.
5. Cox, *The Secular City*, p. 185.
6. Sine, *The Mustard Seed Conspiracy*, p. 136.
7. Ellul, *The Technological Society*, p. 192.
8. Wagner, *The New Pilgrims*, p. 134.
9. One writer recorded that white-collar workers spend 50 percent of their time in that box called an office doing nothing (Barry and Associates, *Greatest Management Principle*, p. 20).
10. See *Charismatic Capitalism* by Biggart, where she writes, "Even the most upbeat corporate culture of traditional American business, however, pales beside the daily round among direct sales distributors" (p. 4).
11. Hendricks and Sherman, *Your Work Matters to God*, p. 27.
12. Osherson, *Finding Our Fathers*, p. 10.
13. Osherson, *Finding Our Fathers*, p. 63.
14. Levinson, *The Seasons of a Man's Life*, p. 334.
15. Hendricks and Sherman, *Your Work Matters to God*, p. 87.
16. Sine, *The Mustard Seed Conspiracy*, p. 136.
17. Hendricks and Sherman, *Your Work Matters to God*, p. 131.

18. Hendricks and Sherman, *Your Work Matters to God*, p. 145–46.
19. Merkle, *Abraham Joshua Heschel*, pp. 22–23.

Chapter 5

1. Gilder, *Men and Marriage*, pp. 62–65.
2. Druck and Simmons, *The Secrets That Men Keep*, pp. 202–3.
3. Frankl, *Man's Search for Meaning*, pp. 130–31.
4. Please don't misunderstand what I'm saying on this point. I believe in counseling and the mental health profession. But I have seen some single men in counseling who need only a kick in the pants, a bear to kill, and a contribution to make. It is hard for some counselors to stop finding problems for which they are needed.
5. Gilder, *Men and Marriage*, pp. 66–67.
6. Knott, "Grief Work with Men," p. 100.
7. Wallerstein and Blakeslee, *Second Chances*, p. 277.
8. Wallerstein and Blakeslee, *Second Chances*, p. 281.

Chapter 6

1. Zilbergeld, *Male Sexuality*, p. 5.
2. Fracher and Kimmel, "Counseling Men About Sexuality," p. 88.
3. Goldberg, *The Inner Male*, p. 119.
4. Fracher and Kimmel, "Counseling Men about Sexuality," p. 91.
5. Goldberg, *The Inner Male*, pp. 231–32.
6. See *Gift of Sex* by Clifford and Joyce Penner for a thorough understanding of the physiology of sexual functioning.
7. Zilbergeld, *Male Sexuality*, pp. 50–51.
8. Of course, the fault in these cases is shared. A marriage takes two committed people, and 95 percent of the time there is shared guilt. Therefore, when a man has an affair, I don't mean to imply that it's the wife's fault. The husband is culpable and responsible for breaching the marriage vow.
9. Dalbey, *Healing the Masculine Soul*, p. 39.
10. Goldberg, *The Inner Male*, pp. 66–67.
11. Statistics quoted in *Women, Psychology's Puzzle* by Rohrbaugh, pp. 271–72.
12. Zilbergeld, *Male Sexuality*, p. 194.
13. Zilbergeld, *Male Sexuality*, p. 172.
14. Taken and adapted from "How to Obtain and Maintain Sexual Intimacy" by Robert and Cinny Hicks, pp. 233–35.
15. Greeley, *Sexual Intimacy*, pp. 118–19.

Chapter 7

1. White, *Parents in Pain*, p. 19.
2. White, *Parents in Pain*, pp. 34, 36.

3. Lamb, *The Role of the Father in Child Development*, p. 25.
4. Lamb, *The Role of the Father in Child Development*, p. 30.
5. Elkind, *The Hurried Child*, p. 182.
6. Elkind, *The Hurried Child*, p. 30.
7. Newman, *Falling from Grace*, p. 139.
8. Newman, *Falling from Grace*, p. 140.
9. Andersen, *Father: The Figure and the Force*, pp. 248–49.
10. Bronfenbrenner, *The American Family* audiotape.
11. Studies indicate that men are spending more time involved in direct parenting than in the past [Pleck, 1985; Gilbert, 1985]. The father's role in child development has only recently come into its own in terms of research. It wasn't until 1986 that Congress became interested in the subject. Thanks to then congressman Dan Coates (Indiana chairman of the Child and Family Committee), testimony was received from researchers. Some of the material has appeared in written form, and some of the researchers have put their conclusions in print. The Family Research Council has made a good attempt to get the word out.
12. Lamb, *The Role of the Father in Child Development*.
13. I know I am oversimplifying American frontier culture. I realize there were dads who were alcoholics or child abusers, dads who gave their kids very little emotional or financial support.
14. Elkind, *The Hurried Child*, p. 199.
15. Appleton, *Fathers and Daughters*, pp. 15–19.
16. Dalbey, *Healing the Masculine Soul*, p. 153.
17. Dalbey, *Healing the Masculine Soul*, p. 159.
18. Dalbey, *Healing the Masculine Soul*, pp. 49–52.
19. Lamb, *The Role of the Father in Child Development*, p. 25.
20. Dalbey, *Healing the Masculine Soul*, p. 54.

Chapter 8
1. Quoted in Dalbey's *Healing the Masculine Soul*, pp. 174–75.
2. Joy, "Is the Church Feminized?"
3. Ford Madison, personal meeting with author, Dallas Seminary faculty meeting.
4. Message given at a pastors' breakfast in Honolulu, Hawaii, January 1979.
5. Dalbey, *Healing the Masculine Soul*, p. 198.

Chapter 9
1. "What Do Men Want?" *Leadership*, Winter 1991.
2. Four—if you count Reconstructionism as a separate group.
3. Blumenthal, *Understanding Jewish Mysticism*, p. 38.
4. Myers-Briggs Personality Inventory.
5. I've been in other men's offices that had a Bible in a prominent place.
6. Heller, *The Soul of a Man*, pp. 79–80.

7. Tanenbaum, *Male and Female Realities*, pp. 77–83.
8. Heller, *The Soul of a Man*, p. 91.
9. Groeschel, *Spiritual Discourses*, pp. 131–32.
10. Kierkegaard, *Christian Discourses*, pp. 113–14.

Chapter 10

1. Moyers and Bly, *A Gathering of Men* audiocassette.
2. Payne, *Crisis in Masculinity*, pp. 12–13.
3. "New Male: Is He Old Hat to Females?"
4. Tanenbaum, *Male and Female Realities*, pp. 12–13.
5. Brown, Driver, and Briggs, *Lexicon of Old Testament Hebrew*. Hebrew *zakar* (male), p. 271; *niqevah* (female), p. 666.
6. Even most homosexual practices affirm this creational purpose. A man must find an opening for his penis, and a woman must find a penis substitute.
7. I realize some readers may not accept my interpretation of the out-of-balance male or issues of personality development. Many persons are content to shrug off these differences as "just the way they are" and forget about trying to see other aspects of their personhood. That approach works well until a man's marriage fails or he loses his job, health, status, and/or money. The loss often gets him into a counselor's office and initiates the process of regarding life in more developmental and novel terms. The loss brings him more in touch with areas of his personhood that have long been denied or discounted.
8. Zilbergeld, *The Shrinking of America*, p. 3.
9. Zilbergeld, *The Shrinking of America*, p. 270.
10. See John 14:17; 16:8–15; Romans 8:16; 1 Corinthians 12:4; Galatians 5:22–23; and 2 Peter 1:2–4 for an understanding of the Spirit's work in the believer's life.
11. Goldberg, *The Inner Male*, p. 259.
12. Goldberg, *The Inner Male*, p. 34.
13. Gilligan, *In a Different Voice*, pp. 28–29.
14. See the chart on summary of differences in Tanenbaum's *Male and Female Realities*, pp. 48, 53.
15. Tanenbaum, *Male and Female Realities*, pp. 72–73.
16. Tanenbaum, *Male and Female Realities*, p. 11.
17. "What Do Men Want?" *Leadership*, p. 40.
18. No mention is made of Joseph after the Lucan account. He had probably died by the time Jesus began His ministry.

Bibliography

Allis, Sam. "What Do Men Really Want?" *Time* special edition, Fall 1990.

Andersen, Christopher. *Father: The Figure and the Force.* New York: Warner Communications, 1983.

Appleton, William S. *Fathers and Daughters.* New York: Berkley Books and Doubleday, 1981.

Barry, Theodore, and Associates. *Greatest Management Principle.* New York: Berkley Books, 1985.

Biggart, Nicole. *Charismatic Capitalism.* Chicago: University of Chicago Press, 1989.

Blitchington, W. Peter. *Sex Roles and the Christian Family.* Wheaton, Ill.: Tyndale House, 1984.

Blumenthal, D. R. *Understanding Jewish Mysticism: A Source Reader,* Vol. II. Hoboken, N.J.: Ktav Publishing House.

Bronfenbrenner, Urie. *The American Family* audiotape, Harvard Seminar Series, 1981.

Brown, Francis, S. R. Driver, and Charles A. Briggs. *Hebrew and English Lexicon of the Old Testament.* Oxford: Clarendon Press, 1907.

Cox, Harvey. *The Secular City*, rev. ed. New York: Macmillan, 1965.

Dalbey, Gordon. *Healing the Masculine Soul*. Waco, Tex.: Word Books, 1988.

Dittes, James. *The Male Predicament: On Being a Man Today*. San Francisco: Harper and Row, 1985.

Druck, Ken, with James C. Simmons. *The Secrets That Men Keep*. New York: Ballantine Books, 1985.

Elkind, David. *The Hurried Child: Growing Up Too Fast Too Soon*. Reading, Mass.: Addison-Wesley Publishing Co., 1981.

Ellul, Jacques. *Technological Society*. New York: Vintage Books, 1964.

Fracher and Kimmel. "Counseling Men About Sexuality." *Handbook of Counseling and Psychotherapy with Men*. Murry Scher et al., eds. Newbury Park, Calif.: Sage, 1987.

Frankl, Viktor. *Man's Search for Meaning*. New York: Pocket Books, 1959.

Gerzon, Mark. *A Choice of Heroes: The Changing Faces of American Manhood*. Boston, Mass.: Houghton Mifflin Co., 1984.

Gilder, George. *Men and Marriage*. Gretna; Pelican Publishing Co., 1986.

Gilligan, Carol. *In a Different Voice: Psychological Theory and Women's Development*. Cambridge, Mass.: Harvard University Press, 1982.

Goldberg, Herb. *The Hazards of Being Male: Surviving the Myth of Masculine Privilege*. New York: Signet Books, 1976.

———. *The Inner Male: Overcoming Roadblocks to Intimacy*. New York: Signet Books, 1987.

Greeley, Andrew M. *Sexual Intimacy*. New York: Seabury Press, 1973.

Groeschel, Benedict J. *Spiritual Passages: The Psychology of Spiritual Development*. New York: Crossroad Books, 1984.

Halverson, Richard. Message given at a pastors' breakfast, Ala Moana Hotel, Honolulu, Hawaii, January 1979.

Heller, David. *The Soul of a Man*. New York: Ballantine Books, 1990.

Hendricks, Bill, and Doug Sherman. *Your Work Matters to God*. Colorado Springs: NavPress, 1987.

Hicks, Bob, and Cinny Hicks. "How to Obtain and Maintain Sexual Intimacy." *Husbands and Wives*. Howard Hendricks et al., eds. Wheaton, Ill.: Victor Books, 1988.

Joy, Donald. "The Innate Differences Between Males and Females." Focus on the Family taped interview with James Dodson, n.d.

———. "Is the Church Feminized?" *Challenge to Evangelism Today*.

Kierkegaard, Soren. *Christian Discourses*. London: Oxford University Press, 1939.

Knott, J. Eugene. "Grief Work with Men." *Handbook of Counseling and Psychotherapy with Men*. Murry Scher et al., eds. Newbury Park, Calif.: Sage, 1987.

Kohlberg, Lawrence. *Essays on Moral Development*, vols. I, II. New York: Harper and Row, 1981.

Lamb, Michael, ed. *The Role of the Father in Child Development*. New York: John Wiley and Sons, 1981.

Levinson, Daniel J., et al. *The Seasons of a Man's Life*. New York: Ballantine Books, 1978.

Lewis, Robert A., and Marvin B. Sussman. *Men's Changing Roles in the Family*. New York: Haworth Press, 1985.

Madison, Ford. From undated notes of personal meeting with author, Dallas Seminary faculty meeting.

Merkle, John C. *Abraham Joshua Heschel: Exploring His Life and Thought*. New York: Macmillan Publishing Co., 1985.

Moyers, Bill, and Robert Bly. *A Gathering of Men* audiotape. New York: Mystic Fire Audio, 1990.

Naifeh, Steven, and Gregory Smith. *Why Can't Men Open Up?* New York: Clarkston N. Potter, 1984.

"New Male: Is He Old Hat to Females?" *USA Today*, December 20, 1990.

Newman, Katherine S. *Falling from Grace: The Experience of Down-*

ward Mobility in the American Middle Class. New York: Vintage Books, 1989.

Nicholi, Armand. *Changes in the American Family*. Family Research Council reprint. Capital Hill: Washington, D.C., n.d.

Osherson, Samuel. *Finding Our Fathers*. New York: Macmillan Publishing Co., 1986.

Payne, Leanne. *Crisis in Masculinity*. Westchester, Ill.: Crossway Books, 1978.

Penner, Clifford, and Joyce Penner. *Gift of Sex*. Waco, Tex.: Word Books, 1981.

Pleck, Joseph H. Article in *Men's Changing Roles in the Family*, Robert A. Lewis and Marvin B. Sussman. New York: Haworth Press, 1985.

Restak, Richard. *The Brain: The Last Frontier*. New York: Warner Communications, 1979.

Rohrbaugh, Joanna B. *Women, Psychology's Puzzle*. New York: Basic Books, 1979.

Scher, Murry, et al., eds. *Handbook of Counseling and Psychotherapy with Men*. Newbury Park, Calif.: Sage, 1987.

Sine, Tom. *The Mustard Seed Conspiracy*. Waco, Tex.: Word Books, 1981.

Smith, David W. *The Friendless American Male*. Ventura, Calif.: Regal Books, 1983.

Tanenbaum, Joe. *Male and Female Realities: Understanding the Opposite Sex*. Sugarland, Tex.: Candle Publishing Co., 1989.

Wagner. *The New Pilgrims*. Palm Springs: Ronald N. Haynes, 1980.

Wallerstein, Judith, and Sandra Blakeslee. *Second Chances: Men, Women and Children a Decade after Divorce*. New York: Ticknor and Fields, 1989.

Wheeler, John. Quoted in "What Do Men Really Want," *Time* special edition, 1990.

White, John. *Parents in Pain*. Downers Grove, Ill.: InterVarsity Press, 1979.

BIBLIOGRAPHY

White House Working Group on the Family. *The Family, A Report to the President*. Family Research Council Publication, undated reprint. Washington, D.C.: Capitol Hill.

Wingren, Gustaf. *Luther on Vocation*. Muhlenberg Press, 1957.

Zilbergeld, Bernie. *Male Sexuality: A Guide to Sexual Fulfillment*. Boston: Little, Brown and Co., 1978.

———. *The Shrinking of America: Myths of Psychological Change*. Boston: Little, Brown and Co., 1983.